BUILDING YOUR GARDEN

BUILDING YOUR GARDEN

IAN PENBERTHY

CRESCENT BOOKS
NEW YORK / AVENEL, NEW JERSEY

Edited and designed by Mitchell Beazley Publishers,
part of Reed International Books,
Michelin House, 81 Fulham Road, London SW3 6RB

Design: *Hans Verkroost*
Editor: *Elizabeth Pichon*
Production: *Peter Phillips, Stewart Bowling*

The publishers have made every effort to ensure that all
instructions given in this book are accurate and safe, but they
cannot accept liability for any injury, damage or loss to either
person or property whether direct or consequential and howsoever
arising. The author and publishers will be grateful for any
information which will assist them in keeping future editions up
to date.

This 1992 edition published by Crescent Books,
distributed by Outlet Book Company, Inc., a Random House Company,
40 Engelhard Avenue, Avenel, New Jersey 07001

Printed and bound in Portugal

ISBN 0-517-07013-8

8 7 6 5 4 3 2 1

Typeset by Hourds Typographica, Stafford
Originated by La Cromolito s.n.c. Milan
Printed in Portugal by Resopal Industria Grafica Lda.

CONTENTS

INTRODUCTION

Any gardener knows that there is a lot more to producing a beautiful garden than planting the right species in the right places. Before you can begin to grow plants, shrubs and trees, the ground must be shaped – worked into the right form. Boundaries must be marked, easy access routes to all parts of the garden laid, levels changed and provision made for the future enjoyment of your labours. As a gardener you need more than just green fingers; you need to be part surveyor, part landscaper, part architect, part construction engineer, part carpenter, part builder and part electrician.

You will need some of the skills of all those professions to create your garden, and since you are unlikely to be able to employ such a variety of craftsmen, you will have no option but to learn those skills yourself. That's not to say that building a garden is a complicated business – it can be, of course, but it doesn't have to be, provided you don't attempt projects that are completely beyond your abilities.

In the process of building a garden, you will have to learn, among many other things, how to mix and lay concrete, how to build walls, how to lay paving, erect fences and hang gates, construct various structures from wood, and possibly even create a pond. It is true that some of these jobs are difficult; others, however, are quite simple, and if you are determined to learn and prepared to practise (and to accept the occasional failure) you will succeed.

Although the construction aspect of a garden may seem less attractive to you than the planting and the rewards of that planting, nevertheless it can be satisfying in its own right. To look at a wall and know that you have built it or a patio and know that you have designed and laid it can be immensely rewarding.

The purpose of this book is twofold. The excellent photographs should inspire you to take a fresh look at your own garden, providing you with plenty of ideas for changes and improvements, while the text and illustrations will describe the basic skills and techniques needed to achieve those ends.

Don't be afraid to try new skills, nor to try again if things don't go quite as you planned. Practice does make perfect – well nearly – and the end result will be well worth the effort.

Happy building!

IAN PENBERTHY

UK/US CONVERSIONS

Throughout this book dimensions are given in metric and imperial units so that they may be of use to readers in both the United Kingdom and North America. Metric units are always given first followed by their equivalent in imperial units.

Where there is a direct conversion, the imperial dimension is shown in parentheses. For example: 25mm (1in). If a standard dimension is being discussed (the minimum size of a fence post, for example) which is different in the UK to the US, the dimensions are given thus: 75mm/4in.

A slash is also used to indicate different terminology describing the same basic item. For example: coping/cap stones, railway sleepers/railroad ties.

WALLS

Walls serve many purposes in a garden – they can provide an impenetrable barrier around the outside of it to stop prying eyes and deter trespassers. Inside the garden, low walls can be used to outline particular areas, such as flower beds and patios, or taller walls can be built to create a safe enclosure for pets and small children, conceal one part from another, or to create a "secret" walled garden.

Walls are particularly popular with the keen gardener for they provide shelter to delicate plants from prevailing winds, and depending on the site will give beneficial shade or alternatively produce sun traps.

When it comes to deciding what material to use to build your wall, there are plenty of options, but whatever you choose, make sure it complements the materials from which your house is built and the overall style of your garden. You might want the formality of brick or reconstituted stone walling blocks, the rambling informality of natural stone, or the geometric precision of pierced screening blocks. Whichever you choose, remember that a well-built wall will last you a lifetime, so think carefully before you start.

Building a wall of any type is a skilled job, which begins with laying a strong foundation, so it is a good idea to practice with secondhand materials in a spare corner of the garden first. When you are confident that you have perfected the necessary skills, you can jump in at the deep end.

A well built brick wall is a major investment in time and money, but it will then last for generations. Here the effects of weather and age are all too apparent, but the wall itself is still strong and its mellow, neglected appearance offsets the rambling plants. The old-fashioned, moss-delineated status evokes a past era of grandeur.

Brick walls

Planning

Some careful planning will be needed before you start building your wall. Where will it be sited? How high will it be? How long? What will it be built from? And, most important, why do you want a wall in the first place?

Other considerations are whether a wall will upset your neighbours or contravene any bylaws. Obviously, a low wall in your garden is unlikely to cause a dispute with the people next door, but a 2m/6ft high brick wall between your garden and theirs, shading their patio from the sun, might just raise a few hackles. Similarly, you may find that there are legal limitations to the height of a wall, particularly if it is at the front of your property. So it will serve you well to ask your neighbours if they have any objections (assuming you are on speaking terms with them – if you are

not, building a tall wall to shut them out of your life may start a full-scale war), and to seek advice from your local planning authority or building department.

As with the construction of many garden features, it is best to start out by making a scale plan on graph paper. Draw in the outline of the garden and put in the major features. Then draw in the wall. This will allow you to measure how long it will be and will show you if there are likely to be any problems with its run. Another way of doing this is in the garden itself, using pegs and cord to outline the wall's position on the ground.

After measuring the wall's length, you can work out how many bricks will be needed to lay one course by dividing the total wall length by the length of the type of brick you intend to use, remembering to make allowance for the mortar joints

– 10mm/½in is the normal thickness for these.

Next, decide on the wall's height and divide it by the brick height (plus joint allowance) to obtain the number of courses needed. By multiplying the number of courses by the number of bricks in each course, you will obtain the number of bricks you need.

However, things are not quite as straightforward as that in most cases. Up to now, we have been considering a course composed of single row of bricks, but unless the wall is only two or three courses high, a single "leaf" of bricks will not really be strong enough and will need reinforcing with piers at regular intervals or by building the wall so that it is staggered or stepped when viewed from above. In addition, it will tend to look insubstantial. A better way of doing the job is to make each course from two

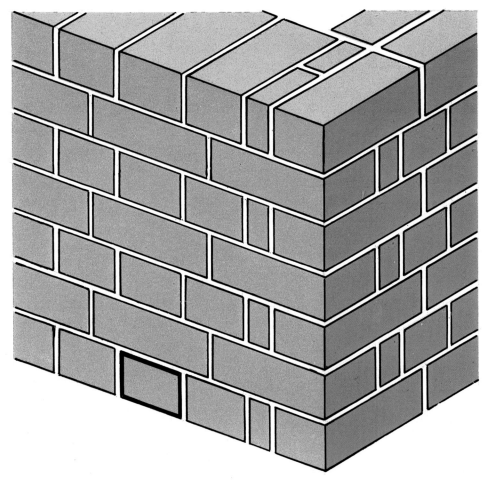

*(**Left and above**) English Bond is popular for garden walls. Bricks are laid with their stretchers (longest sides) and headers (ends) exposed in alternate courses.*

rows of bricks laid next to each other and interconnected to produce a very strong self-supporting structure. This, of course, will double the number of bricks you need.

Even with a single-leaf wall, the courses must be laid so that the bricks produce an overlapping pattern (known as the "bond"). This locks them together, ensuring great strength. However, you will have to cut some bricks to maintain the pattern, particularly at the ends of walls and possibly at corners. If you are lucky you may not waste any when doing this, but you would be wise to add a few more to your total to allow for wastage and any broken ones you find after they have been delivered. Normally ordering an extra ten per cent should cover what you need.

Choosing your bricks

There is a wide range of bricks to choose from in various colours and surface treatments, but if your house is brick built, choose bricks that will match it to give the property a unified appearance, a sense of extending the house into the garden, rather than making the house and garden look like separate areas. This is particularly important if the wall you are building abuts the house.

Even if the house is very old and the exact type of original brick is no longer made, you still should be able to find a modern brick that will blend in. If you search around, you may even be able to find an architectural salvage company that will supply you with secondhand bricks.

Always consult your brick supplier on the type of bricks to use, since many are not suitable for exterior use and may break up when exposed to the elements. Always order enough to finish the job, as you may find the colour of different batches will vary.

When the bricks have been delivered,

(Left and above left) With Flemish Bond, the bricks in each course are laid alternately stretcher-on and header-on.

11

Brick walls

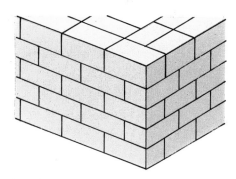

Stretcher/Running Bond is probably the simplest form of brick bond, where the bricks of each course overlap those of the course below by half a brick's length.

With Header Bond the bricks in each course are laid with their headers exposed, the bricks in each course overlapping those below by half a brick's width.

Flemish Garden Wall Bond, uses two or three stretchers for each header in a course. To maintain the bond, queen closers (half-bricks, cut lengthwise) are used at the corners.

A high brick wall makes the ideal backdrop for shrubs and small trees, in this case an apple tree, the branches of which can be trained along the wall. As the brickwork mellows with age and weathering and the shrubbery grows, the two will merge into a delightful barrier between the garden and the outside world. Here, the brickwork is in stretcher/running bond, and all the bricks are laid with their longest sides exposed and the bricks in each course overlap those of the course below by exactly half a brick's length. The wall is topped with a course of bricks laid on end.

stack them carefully (or leave them on their pallets) until you are ready to use them. Cover them with a tarpaulin or plastic sheet to prevent their weathering prematurely, which will cause variations in the appearance of the bricks.

Preparing the foundation

Sound construction is essential when building any wall – not only will the wall be very heavy, putting a high loading on the ground below, but a tall, solid wall will have to withstand considerable pressure from high winds. Sound construction begins with preparing a strong foundation.

The purpose of the foundation is to spread the load of the wall, which is concentrated on a very narrow strip, preventing unwanted settling or rising/heaving in winter, which would weaken the wall and make it dangerous. Normally a foundation consists of a strip of concrete three times the width of the wall and varying in depth depending on the height of the wall. This is called the footing.

For walls up to 600mm (2ft) high, a 100mm (4in) layer of concrete laid on top of a 100mm (4in) layer of well-rammed hardcore (broken brick and rubble) will do, but with anything above that height, 200mm (8in) of solid concrete should be used. However, on light crumbly ground, these figures may need to be doubled, and in this situation you would be wise to seek professional

advice from a local builder or surveyor. Always make sure that the concrete footing is laid below the frost line to prevent rising/heaving in winter. Full details on mixing and using concrete are given on pages 114–117.

The foundation should be marked out with profile boards – narrow wooden crosspieces nailed to pairs of uprights driven into the ground at each end of the wall's run. Nails should be partly driven into the crosspieces to represent the width of the wall. Then extra nails are added to represent the width of the foundation and cords run between them. The edges of the foundation can be marked out simply by sprinkling a line of sand on the ground immediately below the cords.

After removing the cords from the profile boards, a trench can be dug for the foundation. First remove the soft topsoil until you reach the layer of firm subsoil, then dig down to the depth of the foundation. This may mean that two or three courses of bricks will be laid below ground level/grade, but this is essential to ensure that the foundation is constructed on stable ground.

To ensure that the foundation is of uniform thickness, drive pegs at intervals into the bottom of the trench. Each peg should be marked with the depth of concrete (or concrete and hardcore). After driving in the first peg, level the tops of the others to it using a spirit/builder's level and a long, straight length of wood.

English Garden Wall Bond has three courses of stretchers between header courses. Queen closers are also necessary in the header courses to maintain the bond.

English Cross Bond uses half-bats (half-bricks, cut widthwise) in some stretcher courses to vary the bond arrangement, yet maintain its essential interlocking pattern.

Each course in Monk Bond comprises a mixture of headers and stretchers, but queen closers must be used at the corners to ensure the correct bond pattern.

If necessary, adjust the floor of the trench by removing or ramming down extra subsoil until it is near enough level. The pegs can be left in place after the concrete has been laid.

If using a layer of hardcore, ram it down well using a heavy piece of wood,

such as a fence post, but take care not to disturb the level pegs. Then mix the concrete and pour it into the trench, levelling it with the tops of the pegs using a long, straight length of wood. Allow the concrete about a week to harden before laying the bricks.

If you intend to build a wall on a sloping site, the foundation will need to be stepped, and the steps should always be in multiples of the brick height (plus an allowance for the mortar joint). In this case, you will need to erect temporary formwork to hold the concrete in place

A low wall can be given a decorative aspect by laying the outer leaf or side herringbone fashion between brick piers with ties added between the leaves for support.

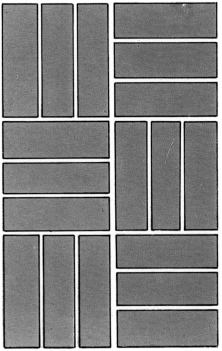

Another decorative pattern for an infill panel of brickwork is basketweave. It must be stressed that these are only suitable for low walls, as they do not produce a strong wall.

Interesting patterns can be made by varying the combination of headers and stretchers, but there is no point to doing this if the wall will be eventually concealed by shrubbery.

Brick walls

(Above) Here a brick is being "buttered" with mortar on its face prior to being used to repair an existing wall. When you are building a new wall, mortar would be spread on the foundation or preceding course of bricks and only the end "buttered." However, the principle remains the same.
(Right) With time, a brick wall adopts a mellow appearance that blends well with rambling greenery.

High and long walls need reinforcing at regular intervals with piers which should be built into the bonding pattern. In this wall, built in a stretcher/running bond, the bricks of the first course of the pier are laid header-on, while to maintain the bond, the second course has one brick stretcher-on, a half-bat and two three-quarter-bats (see opposite).

while it hardens (approximately a week).

Laying the bricks

Before beginning to actually lay bricks, it is a good idea to set out the first course dry, so that you can check the spacing and make any adjustments to ensure the best bonding pattern. Remember to make allowance for the mortar joints.

Next, run a cord between your profile boards to represent the front face of the wall. Mix up some bricklaying mortar (see page 117) and spread a narrow band of it for about 1m/3ft along the foundation from each end or corner of the wall. Hold your spirit/builder's level (or use a plumb line) so that it is touching the cord and absolutely vertical and use a bricklayer's trowel to mark where the level touches the mortar. Do this in several places and join the marks by running the trowel's tip along a straight wooden batten. This will produce a

guide line for laying the bricks. Then remove the cord from the profile boards.

You are now ready to lay your first brick, so take care since the rest of the wall will be built from it. Spread a 10mm/$\frac{1}{2}$in thick layer of mortar at one end, or corner, of the foundation, taking care not to obscure your scribed guide line. Then set your first brick in place, making sure it is correctly aligned and perfectly level. If necessary, tap it down with the trowel handle.

Then lay four or five more bricks, spreading mortar on the end of each one (known as buttering) and carefully butting it up to the one before. Make sure they are all properly aligned and that the course is level. Remove the mortar that squeezes from the joints with the trowel and use it to provide a bed for subsequent bricks. Lay enough for at least two bricks at a time.

Next, spread a bed of mortar on top

of the bricks and lay a second course, staggering the joints to provide the necessary bond. This may mean cutting half bricks if working from a stopped end, or, if working from a corner, reversing the position of the first brick in the course. Continue laying courses in this manner until you have four or five in place with the ends stepped back.

As you progress, check not only that the bricks are level but also that the face of the wall is truly vertical and not bowing. The way to do this is to hold your level at an angle across the faces of the bricks. They should all be in line. If any are not, gently tap them into place with the trowel handle.

To ensure equal joint spacing, it is a good idea to make yourself a gauge rod. This is a length of wooden batten about 1m/3ft long marked off at intervals to represent the height of a brick and its mortar joint. Simply hold the gauge rod against the bricks to check the joint spacing. If necessary, tap the bricks down or add more mortar to the joints to bring everything into line. You can also buy plastic spacers to set into the mortar joints to ensure a uniform thickness.

Next, go to the other end of the foundation and repeat the process for the other end of the wall. If the bricks have "frogs," that is an indentation in one face, lay them so that the frog is uppermost.

Having built up the two ends of the wall, you can fill in the bit in between. Stretch a cord between the ends as a guide for positioning the bricks in each course, moving it steadily up the built-up ends. This should be secured by steel pins, or nails, pushed into the mortar joints between the courses of bricks and aligned with the front edge of the bricks. Check constantly with your level that the courses are horizontal and the face of the wall is vertical/plumb.

If necessary, build up the ends of the wall again and fill in until you reach the desired height of your wall. The mortar joints at the top of the wall should be protected from rain, and there are various ways in which this can be done. The simplest way is to lay a course of bricks on edge, although this will only be feasible if a wall of two leaves of brickwork is being built. Alternatively, there is a wide range of coping/cap stones available.

To cut a brick, chisel a groove around it with a hammer and bolster/cold chisel. Lay the brick frog side downward on a soft surface, such as sand or grass, and deliver a sharp blow to the groove with the bolster/cold chisel. The brick should split cleanly along the line, but may need a little cleaning up.

Cutting Bricks

When building any wall, you will eventually need to cut some bricks to maintain your chosen bonding pattern when you reach the ends of the wall or where piers are added. Cut bricks are known as "bats" or "closers," and the common sizes are shown here. A three-quarter-bat (**top**) will have a quarter of its length removed, a half-bat (**upper middle**) half of its length cut off, and a quarter-bat (**lower middle**) will lose three-quarters of its length. It may also be necessary to cut bricks in half lengthways to maintain a bond across a double-leaf wall where bricks are laid header-on, in which case they are called "queen closers" (**bottom**). Cutting bricks requires practice and confidence with a hammer and bolster/cold chisel, so spend a little time cutting broken or scrap pieces of brick before you attempt the actual job.

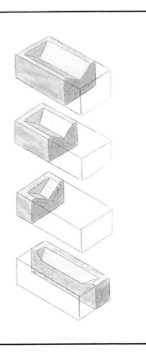

Brick walls

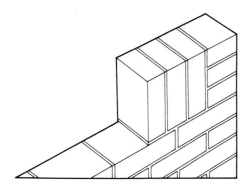

One way in which the top of a wall can be finished off is to lay bricks standing on end or soldier fashion. At the end half-bats are laid on top of each other.

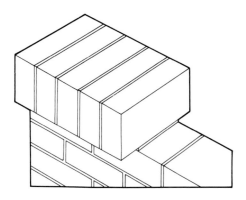

Bricks can also be laid stretcher-up so that they overhang the wall by an equal amount on each side. This will allow rainwater to drip clear of the wall face.

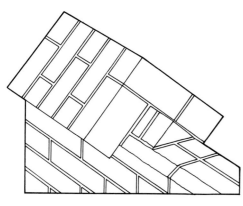

An unusual treatment is to produce a pitched brick coping/capping. However, this requires a wooden framework to support the bricks while the mortar dries.

Strengthening the wall

How the wall is built will determine how strong it is, and this is why the bricks are laid in some form of interlocking pattern or bond. This tends to hold the bricks together, spreading the load. If they were simply stacked one on top of the other with continuous vertical joints, the wall would be very weak. There are various bonds for brickwork and some of the more common are shown on pages 12–13.

Where two leaves of brickwork are used, it is essential to tie the two together for strength. Often the bond is arranged so that alternate courses of bricks span the two leaves to tie them together. However, if the particular bond you want does not allow this, metal or plastic wall ties must be bedded in the horizontal mortar joints to tie the two leaves together.

Additional stability can be given to the structure by building a wall as a series of curves or steps, but the former can be difficult, not only to lay out the curves but also to avoid unnecessarily wide or narrow joints between bricks.
bricks, piers should be incorporated at 1.8m (6ft) intervals, or every 2.8m (9ft) with a double leaf wall. These take the form of a local widening of the wall. Ideally, the piers should be worked into the bond of the wall, but if this seems difficult, they can be built up alongside it and tied in with wall ties. It is essential that you allow for piers when you lay the foundation for the wall.

Finishing the joints

After you lay the bricks, and before the mortar has had a chance to dry, the joints should be finished off or pointed. This involves shaping them so that rainwater will run clear. Simplest is to run the tip of the trowel along the tops of the horizontal joints so that they slope downward. The vertical joints are treated in a similar manner, being angled from one side to the other and blended in with the horizontal joints. Another method is to use a dressing tool or a piece of tubing or hose to produce a concave or recessed joint. Any excess mortar should be removed with a stiff brush.

Stone and concrete walling blocks

There is quite a range of concrete and reconstituted stone walling blocks available, and many are shaped to resemble traditional split stone walling. They come in a wide choice of colours and textures and in various sizes. However, all are laid in much the same way as normal bricks.

Often these blocks only have a patterned finish on one long side and one end, which can cause problems when it comes to deciding on the wall bond. If the wall is to be seen from both sides, then two leaves must be built and linked with wall ties.

Sometimes these blocks have a patterned face formed to look like several stones and have fake joints. In this case, the fake joints must be filled with mortar to match that used to build the wall and finished in a similar fashion.

(Left) Honeycomb bond is ideal for building a decorative, single-leaf screen wall from bricks. The spaces between bricks should be kept to a uniform size – a quarter-bat is best – and, ideally, the gaps in the top course should be filled with cut bricks to give the wall a finished appearance. Here the gaps are a little on the wide side, but since the wall is not very high, this is not critical. A concrete plant container on the top provides added interest, but make sure it is no more than twice the width of the wall, otherwise it will be unstable.

(Below) Pre-cast walling blocks made from reconstituted stone and concrete can make attractive garden walls. The blocks can be quite large and have a patterned face to represent courses of dressed stone walling.

Stone walls

In rural areas, you may find that the natural stone wall with its informal, random appearance fits in much better with the overall theme of your garden than a more formal brick or block wall. However, stone walls require quite a bit more thought than brick or block types, and they require considerably more skill to build properly.

Buying stone

There are several types of stone to choose from – granite, sandstone, field-stone and limestone are popular for walls, although granite is expensive – but if your wall is not to look out of place, always choose a type that is found locally. This is also likely to keep the cost down since you will not be paying for the stone to be transported over long distances.

You can buy stone from stone merchants or mason's suppliers, garden suppliers, and direct from quarries, and you will probably find that you are offered a choice of dressed, semi-dressed and undressed types. Which you choose will depend on the type of wall you want to build and the depth of your pocket. Tell your supplier that you want it for a wall so that he has some idea of the size you will need.

Dressed stone is squared up and cut to the size you specify. It has machined faces to ensure easy jointing and is the most expensive you can buy. Semi-dressed stones are only roughly cut to size and shape and may require final trimming here and there with a hammer and chisel. Undressed stones are just as they come from the quarry – in all manner of shapes and sizes, although the latter should be roughly the same if you ask for it.

In terms of building a wall, dressed stones will be the easiest to use because of their regular shape, and undressed the most difficult for the opposite reason. However, the latter will produce a much more random and informal result.

Deciding on the type of wall

Unless dressed stones are used (which can be worked in much the same way as

(Above) Building a dry stone wall requires a considerable amount of skill if the structure is to be stable and strong. Each face of the wall must slope inward toward the top at a uniform angle. This is achieved with the aid of wooden batter or sloping frames. The side pieces of the batter frames are set at an angle to match that of the wall faces. They are driven into the ground at each end of the wall's run and fixed at the top by crosspieces. Cords are run between the frames to provide a guide for laying the stones. The wall itself is built in a shallow trench on well compacted earth, large flat stones being used as its foundation. More large stones are used to build up each face, while the centre is filled with smaller stones. At intervals, more large flat stones are laid across the wall to tie the two faces together.

bricks and purpose-made walling blocks), building a stone wall requires a considerable amount of skill to produce a sound structure. However, it can be done, provided you approach the job with care and attention to detail. Dressed and semi-dressed stones at least allow some semblance of courses to be laid, whereas undressed stones will need assembling in a random manner to achieve the desired result.

Basically, you have two choices when it comes to the type of construction – you can either "glue" the stones together with mortar as you would a brick wall, or you can lay them dry: this is where real skill is needed if the wall is not to collapse. When dry stone walls are used for agricultural purposes they are constructed completely dry, the stones being laid directly on top of one another. However, when they are used in gardens it is common to bed them directly onto the soil, and fill the joints with more soil so that plants can be grown between the stones. With dry stone walls, the strength of the structure lies entirely with the builder's skill in assembling the stones in a sound interlocking pattern.

Building a stone wall

When building a stone wall, whether the joints are mortared or the wall is built dry, great care is needed in the selection of the stones so that they form a natural bonding pattern and produce a visually appealing arrangement.

In general, larger stones should be

Many types of stone can be used for building walls. This one is built from undressed stones, their varying sizes and shapes producing a wall with rugged, informal appearance.

By contrast, dressed stones have been used for this wall, giving a much more formal, ordered appearance. Dressed stones are the most expensive you can buy, but they are as easy to lay as bricks.

used in the lower layers of the wall and smaller ones near the top. The wall should be built to a "batter," that is, wider at the base than at the top, the sides sloping at an angle of between 1 in 6 and 1 in 10. To assist in achieving a uniform batter along the length of the wall, make up a pair of batter frames, each made from two angled wooden battens secured by horizontal crosspieces at top and bottom so that they match the end profile of the wall. Sharpen the ends of the battens, so that they can be driven into the ground at each end of the wall and cords run between them as guides for placing the stones.

If you intend to build the wall with mortar, you should lay a concrete foundation as you would for a normal brick wall. A dry stone wall, on the other hand, can be built in a trench dug down to subsoil level.

Before beginning the work, it is a good idea to assemble a few stones dry to get the hang of creating a bond and producing the most pleasing appearance. This will be particularly useful if you intend to build the wall dry.

Begin by selecting the largest, flattest stones you have and laying them as foundation stones at the base of the wall, interlocking them as much as possible. Then build the wall up in two leaves so that you can control the appearance of each face.

As with a normal brick wall, you can build up the ends first and then fill in the gap between them. Make sure you keep

Using stones of varying thickness presents difficulties when designing a bonding pattern that will be strong. The builder of this attractive, random-coursed wall, however, has succeeded in this.

When stones are laid dry, real skill is required to provide strength. Close examination shows this split stone wall to have a good bond. Note the method of coping/capping on the left.

Stone walls

within your cord guide lines, raising them as the wall gets higher. Aim for as tight a fit as possible between the stones – you may find it necessary to knock them into shape a little with a heavy hammer and/or chisel. Otherwise, the joints will be weak if the wall is being built dry, and unsightly if being constructed with mortar.

At regular intervals, lay wide flat stones across the two leaves to tie them together, and fill the gap between the two leaves with smaller stones and off-cuts, bedding them in mortar or soil as appropriate.

When the wall has reached the desired height, top it off with more wide flat stones spanning both leaves and then a row of coping/cap stones, all of the same approximate size, stood on edge.

If using mortar to fix the stones together, you can greatly improve the appearance of the wall by using a piece of wood to deeply recess the joints before the mortar dries. This treatment also looks very effective on walls built from dressed stone where the courses are more regular in appearance.

Because of the difficulty in constructing a stable dry stone wall, it is probably best to restrict this type of construction to relatively low walls – certainly no

For added interest incorporate decorative features in your wall. Concrete or stone relief panels can be built in, and niches created to house sculptures or, as here, plant pots and containers. Note the long stone spanning the recess to support the wall above. In a brick wall, you can use angle iron to support the course across the opening, or build a curved arch, using a wooden framework for temporary support.

higher than 1.2m (4ft) – and use the mortar jointing method on higher structures.

Decorative stone panels

Stones can also be used to make decorative infill panels in a predominantly brick wall. This is a particularly effective way of using them, especially if you have a large number of small stones.

The wall itself has to be a double leaf affair, with the rear or inner leaf being all brick. Sections of the outer leaf can then be built from stones mortared together, and these sections or panels could be rectangular or more complex in shape, but must be surrounded by brickwork linked to the inner leaf. Broken flints are ideal for this sort of treatment, but any other small stones are suitable.

(Below) Stone walls make particularly good backdrops for plants. When planted along the top, they can be allowed to trail down the face of the wall, and if pockets of soil are incorporated between the stones, plants can even be allowed to grow from the wall itself. Moss and lichen complete the effect.

(Above) This well-weathered stone wall provides the ideal backdrop for colourful trailing and climbing plants. Some may need a helping hand from well-placed stakes or canes, and string, however.
(Below) Delicate blooms contrast well with the ruggedness of this dry stone wall.

Screen block walls

Designs in Concrete

(**Above**) Precast concrete screen blocks can be bought in a variety of pierced patterns, which can form part of a much larger pattern when laid. Solid "feature" panels are often available, too.

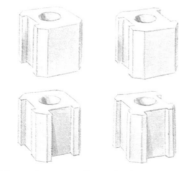

(**Above**) Many ready made designs offer precast concrete pier blocks for strengthening the wall. Slots are provided for the screen blocks in one, two or three sides as appropriate.

(**Above**) Concrete coping/capping stones are available for finishing off the tops of the screen blocks and piers.

A more decorative method of building a garden wall is to use precast concrete screen blocks. These "pierced" blocks come in a wide range of geometric patterns that often form larger designs when assembled into a wall. They have many decorative uses, and are particularly suitable for screening patios to allow cooling breezes and light to filter through. They can be built into low walls to mark the edge of a patio or to divide one section of the garden from another, and they can even be incorporated into traditional brick walls as decorative features. However, because of their open patterns they are not suitable for use in situations where you want a wall to ensure privacy.

Screen blocks are much larger than conventional bricks and one very important difference in the way they are laid is in the bonding pattern. Because their cast-in patterns are designed to make larger patterns when four or more blocks are put together, they cannot be laid in an interlocking bond. Instead, you must use a "stack" bond, with the blocks laid one on top of the other with continuous vertical joints – just the sort of arrangement you really need to avoid when building a wall. Because of this, special measures must be taken to strengthen the wall and its joints. Alignment of the blocks is also critical, otherwise the overall pattern will be affected.

Building a screen block wall

A screen block wall will need a foundation similar to that of a brick wall, but because it will be necessary to dig down to the subsoil before excavating the trench for the foundation concrete, the

Concrete screen blocks make an ideal support for climbing plants, and here a plastic trellis and guy wires have been used to train the stems. Instead of concrete pier blocks, the screen blocks have been built between brick piers and on top of a brick wall, the two materials contrasting nicely.

(Left) Screen blocks have many uses in the garden. Here they have been used to border an archway to another part of the garden. They are built on to a low wall of concrete walling blocks.

first course of blocks is likely to be partly below normal ground level. For this reason, it is common for a screen block wall to be built on top of a low wall of ordinary bricks or concrete walling blocks.

To ensure a strong structure, long uninterrupted runs of screen blocks should be avoided, and vertical piers should be inserted every 3m (10ft) or so along the wall. These are constructed from hollow precast concrete blocks which have slots in their sides to accept the ends of the blocks. For tall walls, these should be reinforced with steel rods or angle iron set in the concrete foundation and running up the hollow middle of the pier, which should be filled with a tamped mortar mix. For this reason, it is important to work out carefully where the piers will fall before laying the foundation concrete. Brick piers can be used as an alternative to concrete blocks.

As with a brick wall, the line of the screen wall can be set out with cords and profile boards. The normal method of construction is to build up about three courses of pier blocks at each end of a section of wall, and then add the blocks

– one at each end at first so that you can run a cord between them to indicate where the others should lie.

As with a brick wall, the mortar joints should be about 10mm/$\frac{1}{2}$in thick, but take great care not to splash mortar on the faces of the blocks as it will stain them. Usually a special white cement is used for the mortar, as normal bricklaying mortar tends to look dirty in contrast to the concrete blocks.

For added strength, strips of wire reinforcing mesh should be laid in every second or third horizontal mortar joint, running it right along the joint and into the mortar joint of the pier.

Most systems of concrete screen blocks include coping/cap stones for both piers and blocks, and these should be used to protect the mortar joints from rain and to give the wall a finished appearance.

FENCES AND GATES

Fences, compared to walls, are quick and simple to erect. But, it is well worth taking some time to work out not only what you want yours to look like, but also what you want it to do. Fencing, entrances and gates should always be incorporated into the overall design of your home and garden whether marking a section of the boundary or all of it, whether partitioning or screening, or whether providing a decorative feature.

Like walls, fences have several uses in your garden, in particular as a barrier around the edge of the property and to divide one part of the garden from another. A tall solid fence will provide privacy, shade, and shelter from the wind, while one of more open construction will allow light and breezes through.

Although not as sturdy and long-lasting as a wall, a fence is much cheaper and quicker to erect, and it makes an ideal temporary barrier while a natural one of shrubs or trees grows to maturity. Even so, a well-built fence can be expected to last for many years, particularly if its wooden structure is treated regularly with preservative.

There are many different styles of fence to choose from, but as with walls it is important to choose the style to match the property. Some, such as picket fences, will look more at home with older properties, whereas others, ranch style fencing for example, will be more suited for use with modern buildings.

A gate is an essential element in a wall or fence if you are to ensure a continuous barrier, yet be able to get from one side to the other without performing a high jump each time. Gates may be of wood or metal, but care should be taken that they fit in with the style of the fencing.

An attractive and sturdy design for a fence, where total privacy is not the main criterion, is the alternate parallel arrangement of solid boards fixed either side of the fence uprights. This is effective as a windbreak, and the gaps between the boards provide informal support for climbing plants.

Fencing

Fence types

There are many different types of fence, so you should have no difficulty in finding one that meets your needs. They fall into two distinct types: open construction and solid. Open-construction fences have gaps between their wooden sections, and while they may be suitable for marking a boundary and, provided the gaps are not too large, restricting the movement of animals and children, they will not provide privacy. Solid construction fences, on the other hand, do just this and will also provide shelter for delicate plants.

Typical open-construction fences include picket, post-and-rail, and ranch-style; solid versions include vertical and horizontal close-boarded/stockade (sometimes with the boards edge to edge, sometimes with feather-edged boards overlapping) and interwoven. Other types of fence include wire link and stranded wire, although neither is particularly attractive and would usually only be used in a garden as a temporary measure until something like a hedge had grown to replace it.

Most types of fence need to be constructed piece by piece on site and can easily be tailored exactly to your needs. However, it is possible to buy ready-made solid fence panels in a range of standard sizes and styles. These speed up construction considerably, but will not be as sturdy as a custom-built fence. In addition, the length of your fence will rarely equal a whole number of ready-made panels, in which case you will have to cut one.

Another type of fence you may find in ready-made form – as a kit of prefabricated parts ready for nailing together – is picket fencing. This, too, will be made to a standard size and may require some trimming to match the length of fencing needed.

Fences must have stout posts, and if these are of wood they should be at least 75mm/4in square for low fences and 100mm/6in square for tall ones. Precast concrete posts are also available, some with slots to accept ready-made fence panels, and both types should be set into the ground by at least 600mm (2ft).

Planning

As with walls, you should plan the position of your fence carefully, either by making a scale plan of your garden on paper or by using string and pegs in the garden itself.

Consider the feelings of your neighbours if you intend to erect a very tall solid fence. Don't forget that there may be bylaws restricting the height to which you may build, so make sure you contact your local planning authority or building department.

Measure the length of your proposed fence and use this plus the height to work out how much material you will need if you intend to build a tailor-made fence. Remember that if you are making a close-boarded fence with overlapping "feather-edge" boards you must allow for the overlap, which can be 13–25mm ($\frac{1}{2}$–1in).

A typical close-boarded/stockade fence panel.

A woven panel with a slatted top section.

A "waney-edge" or horizontal stockade panel.

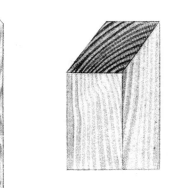

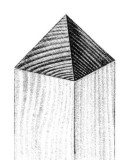

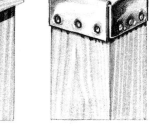

(**Left**) For strength, fence posts should be set in concrete trowelled off to a slope at the top so that rainwater will run away from the post and soak into the ground. Standing the post on a layer of hardcore will prevent its foot from becoming waterlogged.

(**Above**) The tops of fence posts must be protected from rain soaking into the endgrain of the wood. One way is to shape the end of the post so that rain will run off. Soak the cut end with plenty of preservative. Alternatively, a wooden or metal cap can be nailed to the top.

Weathered wood turns an attractive gray.

An unusual treatment for a paling or slat fence.

Fencing

If buying fence panels, simply divide the total fence run by the length of the panel type you intend to use plus the width of one post to obtain the number of panels you will need. Remember, you will need one extra post, unless you intend to fix the end of one panel directly to an existing post or a wall.

Buying fencing materials

You can buy ready-made fencing panels and kits from garden suppliers and timber/lumber yards. The latter will also supply the necessary wood for making your own fencing. In both cases, the wood should have been pressure-treated with preservative – check that the preservative is harmless to plants, as some types are not. For safety's sake never burn scraps of pressure-treated wood or breathe in the dust when cutting it, as it can be toxic. If you are using untreated wood, make sure that the posts are allowed to stand in preservative for a few days before putting them in the ground. This will ensure that their feet are well protected. The rest of the fence can be treated by brush or spray once it has been erected.

When buying nails for fencing work, make sure they are galvanized. This treatment will protect them against rust.

Erecting the posts

Regardless of the type of fence you are building, the posts must be firmly set in the ground. When using fence panels, all the posts can be put in first, but when constructing a tailor-made fence, the posts and any horizontal rails are usually erected at the same time, with vertical boarding or the addition of palings being done last.

First mark out the line of the fence with a cord stretched between two stakes. If using ready-made panels, cut a wooden batten to match the length of a panel so that you can use it as a guide for spacing the posts.

Dig the post holes with either a spade or shovel or with a proper post-hole borer/auger, which you should be able to rent locally. This may well be worth it if you have a lot of holes to dig. When erecting wooden posts, dig the hole a little deeper than the required 600mm (2ft) and fill the bottom with hardcore to allow drainage and thus prevent the foot

The traditional white-painted picket fence – perfect for a cottage garden.

of the post from becoming waterlogged.

Set the first post in its hole, checking that it is aligned with the cord guide line and vertical in both planes with a spirit/builder's level. Stakes driven into the ground at an angle and nailed to the sides of the post will hold it upright while you fill in the hole.

Wedge the post with some hardcore first and then fill the hole with concrete to just above ground level, smoothing it off to a slope so that rainwater will run clear of the foot.

Erect the rest of the posts in a similar manner, checking with a long straight piece of wood and a level that their tops are all in line and level. Then allow the concrete to harden for a few days before erecting the rest of the fencing.

Erecting ready-made panels

If you are using ready-made panels, they are simply nailed between the posts. Prop each panel on bricks or offcuts of wood so that it is level before driving the nails home. You can prevent the panel

With vertical close-boarded fences, it is usual to fit a gravel board between each pair of posts at ground level. This should be nailed to two short pieces of wooden batten nailed to the posts. Its purpose is to protect the bottoms of the boards from rotting through contact with the ground.

When horizontal close-boarded fencing is being erected, or some form of post-and-rail arrangement, you can nail the boards or rails directly to the posts.

edging from splitting by drilling pilot holes for the nails first.

You can also buy U-shaped brackets for nailing to the posts. These allow the panels to be dropped into place and then secured with nails driven through the brackets. Where concrete posts are used, the panels simply slot in from the top.

Most ready-made panels are held together by short, thin nails or even staples, so if one needs shortening it is a relatively easy job to prise off the edging, cut the panel to length with a hand or power saw and nail the edging back on.

Finish the fence by nailing wooden or metal caps to the tops of wooden posts to protect the endgrain from rainwater. Alternatively, the post top can be cut off at an angle so that rainwater will run off.

Tailor-made fencing

With tailor-made fencing, horizontal supporting rails are usually added at the same time as the posts are erected. Known as arris or split rails, they are triangular in section so that water will run off, and their ends fit into slots cut in the posts. The upright palings or boards are then nailed to the faces of the rails.

(Above) "Interference" fencing, which has overlapping boards nailed to alternate sides of the fence rails, provides added depth to a fence and nearly as much privacy as a close-boarded/stockade fence.

(Below) This unusual picket fence is an interesting slant on an old idea.

Gates

Originally designed for agricultural purposes, the field gate has gained domestic respectability and can be seen gracing many a grand drive. Wire mesh pinned across it will prevent pets from wandering.

Choosing a gate

Gates are commonly made of wood or wrought iron, and as with so many other structures in the garden, it is important that you choose one that fits in with its surroundings. A very ornate wrought iron gate would look out of place in a simple country garden, just as a simple picket gate would be inappropriate in an urban courtyard garden.

In general, metal gates should be hung either from metal posts or brick piers, while wooden gates should be used in wooden fences, where possible matching the style of the fence. Wooden gates can also be hung from brick piers, but they will still look a little out of place.

Constructing a gate from scratch is not easy. It must be designed so that the structure will not sag when supported along one edge only. If at all possible, buy gates ready-made, or as a prefabricated kit of parts which can be screwed and glued together.

All gates will need hinges and some form of latch. There is a wide range to choose from to match the style of gate and its material – metal gates will incorporate hinges and a latch, but wooden ones must have them fitted separately.

Where brick piers are used to support the gate, the hinges will be set in the mortar joints between the bricks for strength, whereas with a wooden post they are held in place with screws. Fixing hinges to brick piers with screws and wall plugs is not very satisfactory and is unlikely to provide a strong enough fixing.

Make sure the hinges for your gate are strong enough to do the job and that all the metal fittings (including fixing screws) are rustproofed.

Erecting the posts

If you are using wooden posts for your gate, make sure they are at least 100mm (4in) square if the gate is up to 1m/3ft wide, or 150mm (6in) square if it is wider. Heavy field gates need much larger posts, say 175–200mm (7–8in) square, and may need to be set in the ground by as much as 900mm (3ft). Smaller gate posts need only be set in the

ground to a depth of 600mm (2ft).

Like fence posts, gate posts should be treated with preservative to protect them against rotting, and for heavy gates it is best to use a hardwood such as oak or locust.

Wooden gate posts should be erected in the same way as fence posts with a layer of hardcore at the bottom of the hole and a concrete collar to hold the post in place. Brace them with stakes driven into the ground at an angle while

the concrete sets, making sure they are perfectly upright with a level. A batten cut to match the width of the gate can be used to check the spacing between the posts, which should be just wide enough to allow the gate to swing to and fro easily. Allow the concrete to harden for a week before hanging the gate.

If the ground is soft, it is a good idea to dig a trench between the two posts and fill this with concrete to link the post collars and prevent the weight of the

A selection of country-style gates:
*(**Top left**) On a wide span, two field-type gates may be used, the smaller of the two for pedestrians, removing the need to push open a wide, heavy gate.*
*(**Top right**) This close-boarded/stockade gate helps maintain the privacy afforded by the well-clipped hedge.*
*(**Bottom left**) A simple post-and-rail gate denies access to vehicles.*
*(**Bottom right**) This pristine white picket gate looks quite startling surrounded by the ragged hedge.*

Gates

The formality and painted finish of this unusual fluted gate at the poet Keats' house is not exactly complemented by the weathered fence on each side. The modern lock also mars its appearahce – an object lesson in choosing your gate to match its surroundings. Nonetheless, it is an impressive gate that exudes an air of strength and security.

gate from pulling the hinge post over.

Hanging the gate

First fix the hinges to the gate, then prop it up between the posts, checking that there is plenty of clearance underneath and that it is horizontal. If the gate has a diagonal brace it must run upward from the hinge side to prevent the gate from sagging once hung.

Mark where the hinges are to be fixed to the post, drill pilot holes for the screws and attach the hinges to the post. Fitting the latch is usually quite straightforward, one piece being screwed to the gate, the other to the post. Just take care that they align perfectly.

Building brick piers

When brick piers are chosen to support a gate, you must take great care to align the portions of the hinges that are set into the mortar joints. Probably the easiest way is to attach these to the gate and prop it up while you construct the piers on each side. The hinges will have long "arms" that fit in the joints and may even hook over an adjacent brick.

The piers themselves should be at least 600mm (2ft) square and be built on substantial concrete foundations extending some 600mm (2ft) into the ground.

After care

All types of fencing and gates require regular treatment with preservative or paint if they are to look their best and survive exposure to the elements for any length of time. Hinges and other metal fittings should also be regularly painted after removing any signs of rust and, when fitted originally, the threads of their fixing screws should be given additional protection by dipping them in grease.

Although painting or treating a long fence can be a tedious chore, the reward is a barrier with a more natural, less harsh appearance than a wall. Furthermore, it is obviously easier to change the style of a fence by tearing it down and rebuilding it than it is to remove and replace a wall.

A suburban selection:
(**Left**) Interesting contrasts in these two: the one on the left is neat and well cared for; the one on the right somewhat dog-eared and past its prime.
(**Below left**) Who will let the cat out? This simple gate is in need of repainting, which should be done regularly for all exterior woodwork, otherwise it soon looks shabby. The fixings/hardware should be galvanized, too, as otherwise they will rust and stain paintwork (**right**).

PATHS AND STEPS

Unless you are moving to a newly built home, it is probable that your garden will have at least one path. Redesigning a path and siting steps – if you are lucky enough to have the gradient – can take many happy hours of planning. And it is well worth taking the time so that the end result is both aesthetically pleasing and practical.

Although paths have a practical purpose in your garden, allowing you to move about it without wearing bald patches on the lawn or turning flowerbeds into mud baths, they don't have to look purely functional. They can be made to enhance the overall design, becoming features in their own right.

Paths can be constructed from a variety of materials – bricks, concrete pavers, concrete slabs, cobbles, gravel, concrete, or even sawn logs – and these materials can be laid in many attractive patterns or combined to give interesting variations in texture and colour. In fact, no matter what style of path you choose, you will be able to find a paving material that will suit it, and your taste, exactly.

Constructing a path is quite a simple job to do, regardless of the type of material you pick, but it is important that it is built on a sound foundation or it may subside in places or even break up. Take care to make it level as well, or people may trip and stumble on it with potentially painful results.

Where the level of your garden varies sharply, you will want to incorporate steps in your path. You can normally use the same materials as those in your path to ensure a unified appearance. Building steps is not difficult either, provided you pay attention to their dimensions and make sure they have sound footings.

The focal point in this woodland glade is a miniature pagoda standing atop a broad, shallow flight of steps. The use of tree trunks, pegged firmly in position as each step was excavated, would have involved considerable labour, but the overall effect of the surface chippings and the placing of the rocks and shrubs is beautifully in proportion and "natural."

Paths

Planning your path

Although the shortest distance between one point in your garden and another will be a straight line, that does not necessarily mean that the path you lay between these two points should be straight. A straight path may fit in with a garden that has a rigid geometric design, but in many cases it will serve only to split the garden needlessly in two and would be better if allowed to meander a little.

As with so many garden projects, a scale plan drawn on graph paper will be of tremendous help in planning the position and width of your path. Draw in all the major features and then try different positions for the path. Another way of doing this is to take a photograph of the garden from the house and then use tracing paper to add an overlay showing possible path positions.

If you intend to use bricks or slabs as a paving material, you can sketch these in too and gain a much better idea of how the finished path will look. The pattern in which you lay the paving may require that some pieces are cut, in which case a carefully drawn scale plan of the path will show you just how many will need cutting and allow you to adjust this figure by moving the pattern here and there before actually doing the job.

By drawing in the actual pattern, you will also be able to work out how many bricks or slabs will be needed to pave a predetermined length of path. Then this figure can be multiplied by the overall length of the path to obtain the total number of bricks or slabs required.

As a rule, paths should be about 1m/ 3ft wide, but there is no reason why you can't make them narrower or wider if you wish, provided they are not so narrow that they make you feel that you are walking a tightrope.

Paths don't have to be continuous either – you may prefer to make one as a series of stepping stones across a lawn, which will create less obvious division between one side of the lawn and the other. If you do, however, give great thought to their spacing. If you don't put the steps in the right place, you may end up walking on the grass in between. Also, make sure the steps are slightly below ground level, otherwise you may find that your lawnmower blades become blunt very quickly.

Where paths need to change direction, in general it is better to make that change in the form of a curve rather than of a sharp angle, unless the latter fits in with the overall design of the garden. However, don't go mad with too many curves and squiggles, as building such a path can be a nightmare.

When it comes to laying out the shape of the path, use pegs and cords for the straight stretches and lengths of garden hose for the curved bits.

Constructing the foundation

Any path, no matter what the paving material, needs a sound foundation to ensure stability. This is vitally important, for if the surface begins to break up or becomes very irregular due to subsidence or heaving, the path will become dangerous to walk on, particularly for the old, for the very young, and for everybody at night.

Fortunately, constructing a firm foundation for a path is not difficult, nor does it require the use of concrete (in most cases). Most paths will gain all the strength they need from a layer of well rammed hardcore about 100mm (4in) thick topped with a 50mm (2in) layer of sand.

To prepare the foundation, dig out the area of the path between your guide lines, making the depth of the shallow trench equal to the depth of the hardcore plus the sand plus the thickness of your paving material. There is no need to worry too much about making the path perfectly level along its length, since it is better to follow the ground contours. However, any sharp variations should be levelled out, or dealt with by putting in steps.

Make sure the base of the trench is firm, ramming it down with a stout length of wood such as a fence post. Fill any soft areas with a little rammed hardcore. Then drive a series of pegs into the bottom of the trench, each marked with the depth of the hardcore and sand layers.

Next add the hardcore, spreading it out and ramming it down well. Alternatively, use a garden roller to compact it. Bring the hardcore up to the level marked on the pegs and then add the

Paving stones can be used like stepping stones in a lawn. Mark their outline on the grass before taking out the turf.

Pour coarse stone chippings into each hole to provide a sound foundation for the stones.

Level the chippings off so that each slap sits just below the grass level thus preventing damage to the lawnmower.

sand, raking it out to an even layer. Remove the guide pegs and fill in their holes before laying the paving.

Small paving materials, such as bricks and pavers, need some form of curb at the edges of the path to prevent them breaking away. Bricks stood on edge can be used for this, or you can lay precast concrete curb stones. In many cases, the curbs can simply be bedded in sand like the paving itself, but if the ground is soft, it is better to set them in concrete, which should be done before the sand is laid. The tops of the curbs should be slightly below the surface of the paving so that rainwater will not be trapped on the path.

Laying bricks and pavers

Bricks can produce very attractive paths and are particularly suitable for older properties and gardens. However, when you buy them make sure you tell your supplier that they are to be used for a path, as many bricks are not durable enough for this use, and break up under the action of damp and frost. Second-hand bricks are often ideal for paths because their weathered appearance makes a new path look as though it has been there for a long time.

Bricks can be laid on edge or on one face, and if one face has a frog (an indentation), this should be laid downward. Some types of brick may have two frogs, but these should not be used for paving, unless laid on edge, as they will produce an uneven surface. Bricks with holes running right through them should also be laid on edge.

Pavers are often similar to bricks in appearance, but they are made from concrete and are available in a wide range of colours. Complex interlocking shapes are also made to provide interesting patterns in the finished path. Many pavers have a plain flat surface, while others have bevelled edges or a surface with a regular raised pattern to provide a non-slip finish. Sizes and thicknesses may vary considerably.

With bricks or plain pavers, you can improve the appearance of a path by laying them in a pattern, and among the

Brick is a marvellous paving material, since it mellows to delightful muted shades, blending well with many styles of garden. Here, bricks have also been used as curbs along the edge of the path.

Paths

typical arrangements are herringbone and basketweave. The latter, however, will require quite a lot of cut bricks at the edges and, being small, these pieces must be retained by a curb.

Bricks and pavers can be cut by first making a groove all the way round with a bolster or cold chisel and hammer. Then lay a straight piece of wood under the groove and strike the waste side of the groove with the hammer handle. Alternatively, a hydraulic stone cutter can be rented if you have a lot of cutting to do.

When laying the bricks or pavers set them out in your desired pattern, keeping the gaps between them uniform and no more than 10mm/½in wide. After you have placed a few, lay a wooden straightedge across them and tap it down with a heavy hammer until the faces of the bricks or pavers are all level.

Ideally, if the path does not run downhill naturally, you should arrange a slight drainage "fall" or "pitch" to one side or the other of the path so that rainwater will run off. Check this with a level laid on top of a second straightedge held across the path. A small wooden wedge underneath one end of the level will allow you to obtain a consistent fall by keeping the level's bubble in the middle of its tube. Tap the bricks or pavers down more on the side to which the rainwater must drain, but make sure the

(Above) Because bricks are relatively small, they offer a lot of scope for laying patterns. Some form of woven or bonded effect is often chosen, but here they are laid in widely spaced, straight courses in a gently sloping path. The bricks are set in concrete, which is essential when they are so widely spaced.

(Below) The small size of bricks also allows them to be used for curved paths. Here, they have been laid in an overlapping bond pattern and the gaps filled with soil, encouraging the growth of moss. This should not be allowed to spread over the bricks, however, as it will make the path slippery.

tops of all the bricks still remain in line.

Another method of setting the bricks or pavers in position is to use a mechanical plate vibrator which applies pressure to the paving and shakes it to set it firmly in the sand bed. This type of equipment can be rented and is worth having if you are laying a large area of these small blocks.

Once all the bricks or pavers have been laid and compacted, the gaps between them can be filled. With such small blocks there will be a lot of gaps and while you could use a fairly dry mortar mix, it would take a long time to do the job. Much easier is to spread sand over the paving and brush it into the gaps with a broom, but this may need adding to occasionally if any is washed away by particularly heavy rain.

You could also fill the gaps by brushing in a dry mortar mix and either spraying it with water from a watering can or waiting for it to rain. The mortar would then set hard, but this method is not very satisfactory and may lead to considerable staining of the surface.

Stone setts/agate and cobbles

Setts/agate are rectangular blocks of stone, often granite, which have a rough surface but can be used for paving, although they would be better as decorative inserts rather than the sole paving material. They come in various sizes and can be laid in much the same way as bricks and pavers. However, the gaps between them should be partially filled with gravel and then topped with mortar. This should be finished off to just below the surface so that the top of the sett/agate stands proud.

Cobbles are naturally rounded stones which have been shaped by the action of water. They come in a range of sizes from 25mm (1in) upward. They are not the easiest of surfaces to walk on but, like setts/agate, can be used as decorative inserts to break up a large area of paving.

Cobbles should be pressed into a layer of concrete laid on top of your prepared sand and hardcore base. Pack them close together so that little of the concrete is

visible, and gently tap them down with a length of wood to ensure that their tops are all level. They should protrude no more than about 10mm/½in.

You can arrange cobbles in a random fashion, or lay them in courses. If they are fairly flat, they can all be laid on edge for an unusual finish.

Using paving slabs
Precast concrete paving slabs are another popular means of making a path. They are available in a variety of shapes and sizes and in a range of colours, allowing you to mix them to produce varying patterns.

An important point to remember when using paving slabs is that they are very heavy, so take care when lifting

(Left) These widely spaced cobbles set in concrete would be uncomfortable to walk on, but they make an attractive edging to a path.
(Below left) Much easier to walk on are these flat pebbles set just above the level of the concrete.
(Below right) Flat pebbles set on edge can be laid in many geometric patterns.

Paths

them always to bend your knees and keep your back straight. Alternatively, "walk" the slabs to where they are required. Wear heavy shoes to protect your feet and thick gloves if the slabs have a roughcast finish.

Laying slabs can be done in much the same way as laying bricks and pavers. However, it is more usual to provide a gap between them of 9–13mm ($\frac{3}{8}$–$\frac{1}{2}$in), or even more if you live in an area that experiences extreme variations in temperature throughout the year. To ensure a uniform width to the gaps, cut short pieces of thin wooden batten to act as temporary spacers.

Although slabs can be laid satisfactorily on sand, a path that will receive heavy use may be more stable if you set the slabs on mortar pads laid on top of the foundation's sand layer. Depending on the size of the slabs, lay three or four pads for each slab, lower the slab into place and tap it down with the handle of a heavy hammer. Check for level, removing or adding mortar if necessary.

(*Top*) Bricks and paving slabs can be combined to good effect for a formal path. Lay the bricks first as they need a deeper foundation, then the slabs.
(*Above*) Here an attractive path has been created with different colours and sizes of slab.
(*Right*) Slabs are not so versatile for laying curving paths, but they work with triangular fillets of mortar or gravel.

When the slabs have been laid, you can fill the gaps between them with sand or use a very dry crumbly mortar mix, trowelling it off neatly.

If you need to cut slabs to fit in with your laying pattern, do so in the same way as cutting bricks and pavers, although you may find it easier to keep working the chisel back and forth along the groove until the slab parts. Cut the slab on grass or a bed of sand that will absorb the shock of the hammer blows.

Gravel and asphalt paths

The use of gravel as a paving material can be very effective in many styles of garden. Furthermore, it is easy to lay and easy to maintain. However, you must take steps to restrict the tiny stones to the pathway by providing some form of positive edging, such as bricks laid on edge or concrete curb stones bedded in sand or concrete, or even stout preservative-treated boards secured by stakes driven into the ground.

To lay a gravel path, replace the sand layer in your foundation with a 50mm (2in) layer of coarse gravel and roll it well to compact it. Then add a 50mm (2in) layer of fine gravel, raking it out level and rolling it again to make a firm surface.

Although asphalt is more commonly used on driveways, it can also be used for paving and is particularly suitable for resurfacing an old path, provided the original paving is in sound condition. Cold-cure asphalt is available in a choice of colours and is relatively straightforward to lay.

Basically, after the original surface has been swept clean, a bituminous sealer is brushed over it and allowed to cure partially. Then the cold-cure asphalt is raked out to a depth of about 25mm (1in) and rolled well to compact it. Keeping the roller wet will prevent it from picking up particles of asphalt as you work.

Usually, contrasting coloured stone chippings are supplied with the asphalt and these can be scattered over the surface to improve its appearance prior to a final roll. Asphalt does not need any

edging to restrain it, but it will look a lot neater if you lay raised curb stones along each side of the path.

Another method of resurfacing an existing path is to apply bituminous sealer and then scatter stone chippings directly on top of it, rolling them down to compact them.

Crazy paving

Often garden suppliers and stone merchants will sell broken stone and concrete slabs at considerably less than the cost of whole slabs, and these broken pieces can be used to good effect to make crazy paving. However, unlike whole slabs, crazy paving does need a bit more

Gravel and stone chips make versatile paving materials for informal settings. Rake them out to a depth of about 50mm (2in) on a hardcore foundation and roll well to compact the surface. Curbs are essential to prevent the gravel or chips from spreading but these can soon be disguised by careful planting to retain the informal appearance of the path. Here the paving blends well with the stone steps, seat, and wall.

Paths

thought when it comes to laying out the pieces to obtain a pleasing arrangement and to keep the gaps to a minimum.

It is important to position larger pieces along the edge of the path and to put the smaller ones in the middle. If the small pieces are at the edges they may break away unless you have laid curbs.

Bed the pieces of broken slab in the normal manner, but because the gaps between them will inevitably be larger than usual, these must be filled with mortar. Carefully trowel this off flush with the tops of the stones.

Sawn logs for paving

An unusual material for paving is wood in the form of sawn logs which, when set on end, provide an interesting pattern of circular shapes. The logs should be cut into 150–200mm (6–8in) lengths and should be left to soak in preservative for several days before laying.

Instead of a normal path foundation, spread a 75mm (3in) layer of coarse gravel across the bottom of the path trench and set the logs in this, tapping them down and twisting them to and fro to bed them firmly. Check that their tops

(Below) Broken stones set like stepping stones in a surround of gravel work well in this rambling country garden.
(Below left) Traditional crazy paving uses broken slabs set in mortar, but remember to keep the gaps as narrow as possible.

42

are level by laying a straightedge across them. Then fill the gaps between the logs with more coarse gravel until it is flush with the tops of the logs.

By using a range of different size logs, you can keep the gaps between them to a minimum.

Looking after your path

Paths need looking after if they are to retain their appearance and provide safe walking, for, over the years, they will be subjected to attack by rain, frost, ice, the sun, and weeds.

Pull out weeds as soon as they appear and prevent their reappearance by treating with weedkiller at least once a year. Moss and algae growth, which is encouraged on a damp path, can be dealt with in a similar manner, using a moss killer and fungicide.

Cracks and holes in concrete paths should be opened up with a cold chisel and repaired with fresh mortar, while crumbling edges can be repaired in the same way, using a board to provide a temporary support to the mortar while it hardens. Where bricks or pavers have broken up, chop them out with a cold chisel and insert a replacement.

(Above) Sawn logs make surprisingly durable paving material when set on end in gravel.
(Above left) Split stones can be set on edge for paving, too. Lay them in courses, keeping their tops level.

Steps

Where your path meets abrupt changes in the level of your garden you will have to put in a flight of steps. You have two basic choices as to the type – either freestanding against a vertical surface, such as a retaining wall, or built-in where the steps are cut into a slope. The former is a much more formal arrangement, whereas the latter has a more natural appearance.

Whatever type of steps you decide to build, there are some important points to bear in mind regarding their dimensions. For a start, you must make sure that all the steps in the flight have the same dimensions, otherwise they will be difficult to walk on and may cause people to stumble and fall. They should not be too steep, nor too shallow as this will also cause problems.

Ideally, the risers (the vertical portions of the steps) should be between 100 and 150mm (4 and 6in) high and the treads at least 300mm (1ft) from front to back. The treads should also be at least 600mm (2ft) wide and where they are made from something like concrete paving slabs, the front edge should over-hang the riser by about 25mm (1in) to allow water to drip clear. All treads should also have a drainage fall/pitch toward the front edge.

Steps can be constructed from a wide variety of materials, but it is best to match those already in use in the garden. Bricks and concrete or stone walling blocks are ideal for the risers, and the treads can be made from most paving materials, so you can make them look like a continuation of an existing path, rather than an afterthought that was suddenly included.

(Above) This flight of steps uses bricks for the risers and precast concrete paving slabs for the treads. The coloured slabs have weathered somewhat and the tones blend quite naturally with their surroundings. The stones used to retain the adjoining flowerbeds and the plants themselves soften the edges of the steps so that they are less obtrusive.

(Right) Blending well with its surroundings is this flight made from dressed stone blocks. Allowing plants to grow between the stones softens their stark appearance. However, one drawback of these particular steps is that they are of different heights, which could cause someone to trip or stumble.

(Left) Seeming to float in a sea of foliage, these steps are made from large stone slabs with a semi-dressed surface that provides an interesting texture and one that will be slip-resistant. Such stones are expensive, but may be worth the expense for their natural appearance. The risers are of brick, but the slabs do not fit right back against them. Instead, a narrow bed of soil runs between the back edge of the tread and the riser. This is planted with low ground-cover plants that grow to just sufficient height to disguise the risers completely.
(Below) Bricks are as suitable for steps as they are for paths and, as here, allow brick paths to be continued to different levels of the garden. In this instance they lead to a wooden deck. However, some attempt at bonding the bricks must be made to ensure a strong structure.

Building freestanding steps

In addition to risers, freestanding steps require side walls to support the edges of the treads. Where they are built against an existing wall, you should use matching materials to give a unified appearance. The step walls should also be tied into the existing wall in some way; either by chopping out sections of brick from the existing wall with a hammer and bolster/cold chisel and "toothing" in the step walls, or by drilling holes in the mortar joints and bedding 150mm (6in) nails in them and the step joints as the steps are built.

For a low flight of steps – say four treads – the side walls and bottom riser can be built on a strip of concrete 100mm (4in) deep and twice the width of the materials used for the walls. But above that height, they should have a concrete slab foundation covering the entire area of the step base, again 100mm (4in) deep.

Mark out the positions of the first riser and side walls with cords and pegs or profile boards as you would for a normal wall and then build up to the level of the first tread. Allow the mortar to harden slightly and then fill the area within the riser and side walls with compacted hardcore, making sure it is flush

Steps

When building a flight of steps, the first job is to outline their position using pegs and cords. Measure the height of the slope and work out how many steps will be needed. You may need to add or remove soil at the top to ensure a uniform riser height.

In this instance, the slope is a shallow one and the flight of steps short, so the entire area of the flight can be dug out to the lower ground level and the steps built as a freestanding flight. On a steeper or longer slope, it is more practical to dig out the individual step shapes in the bank and then add a layer of hardcore.

Lay a concrete foundation for the steps over the well-rammed hardcore. Then, when this has hardened, begin laying the bricks. Lay the perimeter course first and decide whether you will build each riser on the tread below or build up the riser from the foundation, as here.

A flight of steps set into a grassy bank can look very effective, even when not linked to a path. These have been used as an unusual planter.

Fill the "boxes" formed by the riser walls with rammed hardcore. Take care when you do this not to disturb the brickwork, as the mortar will still be weak. Set the paving-slab treads on beds of mortar and make sure they have a slight fall/pitch toward the edge or "nose" of the step to prevent rainwater from collecting.

with the tops of the walls and riser.

Next mark the position of the second riser with cords, lay a 10mm/½in bed of mortar across the hardcore and build the riser and side walls up to the level of the second tread. Backfill again with hardcore. Continue in this way until you have built all the risers and the side walls are finished. Take great care not to dislodge anything when you are ramming in the hardcore.

Finally, bed the treads themselves on a solid layer of mortar spread over the hardcore or pads of mortar if using paving slabs. Fill the gaps between the paving slabs with more mortar.

For tall flights of steps with five treads or more, you must provide extra strength by building each riser directly from the foundation so that the structure resembles a series of boxes, each of

The finished flight of steps. Adding plants along the edges of a flight is a good idea and helps soften the straight lines and "sharp" edges of the slabs. With time, the steps take on a more natural appearance.

Steps

which must be filled with well-rammed hardcore.

Tackling built-in steps

In fact there are two ways in which you can set a flight of steps into a sloping bank. One is to dig into the bank so that you can, in effect, build a set of free-standing steps (with their own back wall) and then backfill around them. This is okay for a low flight, but would involve a lot of digging out if the bank was a tall one – not only that, the walls of the steps would need to be built very strongly to resist the pressure of the ground around them.

The other method is simply to cut the step shapes into the bank, ram in a layer of hardcore as a foundation for each tread and build each riser on the back of the tread below it. With this method all that is necessary is to lay a 100mm (4in)

(Above) An unusual combination of materials and textures. Heavy sections of lumber have been used to make wide steps joining brick terraces. Railway sleepers/railroad ties could be used in the same way.
(Left) More formal is this flight of steps and retaining wall built from concrete walling blocks with paving-slab treads.

strip of concrete at the base of the steps as a foundation for the first riser.

You may find that the height of your bank does not quite match a whole number of risers and treads, in which case you may have to remove soil from the top, or possibly add some, making sure it is well rammed down.

Building steps in this manner requires a lot of careful marking out with cords and pegs. You will need not only cords to mark out the sides of the flight but also cords at right angles to these to indicate the exact position of the front edge of each tread.

Log steps

Another method of constructing built-in steps which is ideal in a rambling, country-style garden is with wooden logs. These should be cut to the width of the steps and left to soak in preservative for several days before laying them.

Cut out the step shapes in the bank as before and use the logs to form risers secured by wooden stakes driven into the ground. Fill in behind the logs with a layer of well-rammed hardcore and then add a 50mm (2in) layer of gravel on top of that to form the tread, which should be slightly lower than the top of the log to prevent the gravel spilling over the edge.

Old wooden railway sleepers/railroad ties could also be used in this way.

Take care where you use this type of step, since the gravel could cause snow and ice to accumulate during the winter. Therefore, it is best used to provide access to parts of the garden that will not need to be reached during the winter months.

Safety considerations

Take care when planning a flight of steps to make sure that they are safe to walk on, particularly if they will be used by the old or very young. Don't make them too steep, so that they are tiring to climb, nor too shallow, as that increases the risk of tripping. On a long flight, add a landing halfway up, which will reduce the distance someone will fall if they do stumble.

A wooden or metal handrail is a sensible safety precaution, as is outdoor lighting to illuminate the steps if they are likely to be used after dark.

Regular maintenance will ensure that the steps are safe to walk on. Treat them with a fungicide to prevent algae growth which would make the treads slippery, and remove moss and weeds as they appear. Chop out crumbling bricks and replace them with fresh ones, and if the treads become loose, rebed them on fresh mortar, turning them if necessary to disguise broken or worn edges.

Steps don't always have to be practical; they can be used to guide the eye to some decorative feature, such as a statue or piece of garden architecture, as they have been here in this oriental-style garden.

PATIOS AND COURTYARDS

Having a well laid out and attractively planted garden is fine, but to get the most from it you should be able to spend time relaxing in it as often as the weather permits. One way in which you can do this is to build a patio or a walled courtyard.

A patio will provide you with somewhere to sit in the sun, dine outdoors, and entertain friends in comfort, and it will make the garden as essential a part of your life as your house itself.

Patios can be constructed from many different materials – practically all types of paving are suitable, as is wood – to complement the construction of your house and blend in with the overall theme of your garden. They can range in style from a simple paved square to a complex "mini garden" on various levels incorporating planters, screens, a built-in barbecue and seating, and even an ornamental pond.

The patio treatment can also be extended to a small walled courtyard with great effect, turning it into an outdoor living room.

A desire for an area of rest and relaxation has inspired this peaceful patio design. Informality is the keynote here, with devices such as raised beds ensuring minimum maintenance, and all-weather garden furniture that can stay put all the year round.

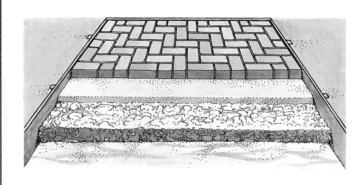

Patio foundations

A large area of paving such as a patio needs a firm foundation if the surface is to be stable and not to sink or heave. This means digging down until you reach firm subsoil, then adding a 100mm (4in) layer of well-compacted hardcore across the site. This is topped by a 50mm (2in) layer of sand which should be raked and rolled level. Finally, the paving can be laid on top of the sand and tapped down level. Some form of curb will be needed around the edges of the patio – unless the patio abuts existing walls – and can be made of precast concrete, brick, or some other suitable material. The joints of this brick paving have been filled with mortar, which is time consuming but it does prevent weeds from growing between the bricks. Sand can be used instead but may need occasional weeding.

Masses of colourful plants tumbling down a rockery and overflowing from pots make this patio a delightful place in which to relax. The plain paving slabs and weathered brick path are perfect for this setting.

With such a large area of these small blocks, it will definitely pay to rent a plate vibrator to set them firmly into the sand bed. To protect the surface of the bricks or pavers, make sure the vibrator comes with a rubber sole plate, or use something like a piece of sacking.

Fill the gaps between the bricks or pavers by spreading sand over the patio and brushing it in with a broom.

If paving slabs are chosen as the surfacing material for the patio, you can bed them either directly on the sand or on pads of mortar as with a path. Use strips of wood as spacers between the slabs and fill the gaps between them with sand or a very dry mortar mix which should be carefully trowelled off flush with the surface of the slabs. A large area such as a patio will allow you to experiment with different colours of slabs and different shapes to obtain varying patterns in the surface.

One way in which you can check whether all the slabs are level with each

other is to stretch a cord across the surface. Provided it is held taut it will show up any that are low or high. These slabs should be lifted and sand or mortar added beneath them or removed.

Sunken patios

Of course there is no reason why your patio should be restricted to one level, and if you have a sloping garden (either away from the house or toward it), you can build your patio on two or more levels, which allows you a lot more range in planning such features as built-in seating, planters and steps.

With a sunken patio, try to make use of the contours of the ground as much as possible as this will save you from excavating vast amounts of soil. The construction should be carried out in tiers – which can all be marked out in one operation using cords and pegs – beginning with the lowest point, which should be surfaced in the normal manner. Each raised level should be bordered by a

retaining wall (see page 60), and each can be backfilled with soil and hardcore before paving that particular level.

Where the slope of the ground is shallow, you can construct wide terraces that double as both steps and informal seating or surfaces on which you can display potted plants. In some cases, you may prefer to omit the paving, add some form of coping/capping to the retaining wall and make a planter instead.

On steep slopes you have the option of building several narrow tiers or planters, or possibly constructing a tall retaining wall with a planter at the top or a surface for pots.

Patio drainage

Depending on the lie of the ground, sunken patios may be bordered on all sides by terraces, or may be open on one or more sides. This can have an important effect on drainage.

Obviously, a patio that has terraces all around it will soon become a pond or a

Coloured precast concrete paving slabs shaped to resemble panels of smaller bricks or pavers can be very effective if used carefully. To complete the ruse, their "joints" should be filled with mortar. I don't think they work as well when they are used as treads for steps, however.

Patios and courtyards

swimming pool after a heavy downpour, unless you provide some form of drainage. This is particularly critical if the patio adjoins the house and the natural slope of the garden is down toward it. An open-sided sunken patio, on the other hand, can be given a drainage fall/pitch toward the open side so that water will run off it naturally.

Good surface-water drainage is an important aspect of all patios, and it can usually be taken care of by arranging a simple drainage fall/pitch toward the garden. Never allow the patio surface to slope toward the house.

With a very large patio, or one that is built on several levels, it is better to take some more positive steps toward disposing of rainwater. This means laying a drainpipe from the lowest point on the patio to a soakaway/dry well somewhere in the garden. Obviously, this should be laid in before the patio foundation is completed, since the pipe will have to run below it.

Basically you have two choices when it comes to drainage: you can either install a drain in the middle of the patio, or at a corner or to one side linked directly to the pipe and with the patio surface sloping toward it; or you can construct a concrete gutter along one side (you can buy precast gutter sections) with the drain at one end or in the middle and, again, the patio surface with a fall/pitch toward the gutter. The drain itself should come with a metal or plastic grid, which should be set about 25mm (1in) below the patio surface. Pre-cast concrete gutter sections can also be fitted with metal grids, but if this looks too functional, you can fill the gutter with large pebbles or broken stone. These won't stop the flow of water, but will make the gutter look less obvious.

The pipes can be normal plastic or glazed stoneware versions, or you can use special land-drainage pipes which are simply butted together rather than being positively joined. They should be laid in a gravel-filled trench topped with soil.

The soakaway/dry well can be a simple pit about 1.2m (4ft) in diameter and 1.5m (5ft) deep which should be

A well aged patio using a combination of large square stone slabs and concrete pavers in a checkerboard pattern and bordered by a dressed-stone wall. Foliage is beginning to encroach upon it, which can be very attractive, removing the sharpness and regular lines of the masonry. The bright colours of the flowers lift the subdued tones of the paving and wall, while the statues focus the eye.

filled with rubble to within about 300mm (1ft) of normal ground level/grade. The drainpipe should be laid to the middle of the soakaway/dry well and obviously terminate near the top. Thus water from the pipe can percolate down through the rubble and gradually drain away through the soil. Spread a strong plastic sheet or building paper over the top of the rubble before replacing the topsoil as this will prevent the soil from being washed down through the soak-away/dry well and filling it with silt.

Wooden decks

Another method of providing an area for sitting and sunning or dining al fresco is to build a wooden deck, which may be in greater harmony with the surrounding garden than a harsher-looking hard-surfaced patio. Although a deck needs more looking after (with regular treatment with preservative), it will be easier to build than laying a normal patio.

Again a sound foundation is necessary for a wooden deck, and here it takes the form of low brick walls or concrete piers about 300mm (1ft) high and spaced at about 1.2m (4ft) intervals across the site. For neatness, it is a good idea to build a continuous peripheral wall too, so that the underside of the deck is not accessible to pets and small, inquisitive children. The tops of the walls should all be level with each other as they provide the supports for the deck's main supporting joists. These are cut from wood measuring at least 100mm (4in) square. It is important that the surface of the deck remains at least 150mm (6in) below the house damp-proof course to prevent damp penetrating the walls.

The joists simply rest on top of the low walls, but there must be some form of damp-proof course (such as bituminous felt) beneath them to prevent damp rising up through the brickwork and attacking the wood. They can then be decked with boards about 25mm (1in) thick and virtually any width you care to use, depending on your preference. Remember to leave narrow gaps between the boards for drainage. They are held in place by galvanized nails

50mm (2in) long. All the wood should be pressure-treated with preservative. If you are not happy with the natural light tone of the wood you may be able to buy it pre-stained in a range of colours or you can stain it yourself.

Courtyards

Houses with small walled yards can make great use of the many features of a patio to produce attractive paved courtyards that are easy to construct and maintain.

Different types of paving can be combined to give variations in colour and texture. Walkways, for example, can be laid in brick or paver, while the remainder can be surfaced with paving slabs. Raised planters can be added in strategic positions to add colour and a change in level, while a small wooden deck will provide a contrast in surface and possibly a natural link with another feature such as a tree.

Courtyards need careful planning to avoid their becoming overwhelmed by too many clever ideas. Wherever possible features such as planters, shrubs and screens that will prevent the entire courtyard being seen from any one position should be incorporated to disguise or conceal the yard's small size.

(Above) Wooden decks are an effective way of constructing a patio that is in harmony with its surroundings. Provided the wood is treated with preservative and galvanized fixings/hardware are used, a deck will last a long time.
(Below) Omitting slabs from a patio will provide useful planting areas.

PLANTERS AND RAISED BEDS

Terracing is the oldest form of landscaping. Anyone visiting the mountainous areas from the Mediterranean to the Far East will have wondered at the endurance of those ancient dry stone walls. They were built to conserve precious soil for crops, with little thought for artistry, but we can construct raised beds ourselves and we can design them specifically to enhance the shape of even quite tiny gardens.

If the ground in your garden slopes, you may prefer to divide it into two or more distinct flat terraces linked by steps with raised flower beds providing the necessary division between each pair of terraces. Although this will alter some of the natural appearance of the garden, it will assist in forming distinct areas which can be treated in different manners or styles to suit your needs or whims (a patio, lawn area, vegetable garden and so on).

To produce these flat terraces, it will be necessary to construct earth retaining walls to hold back the ground of each upper level, thus preventing it from spilling on to the level below. These are built like any other walls

except that care must be taken that they are strong enough to hold back the quite considerable pressure of the soil behind them.

You will also need to construct retaining walls if you want to build raised planters. These are basically large boxes filled with soil, and are ideal on patios and in courtyards to provide a visual change in level and to allow trailing plants to be used to good advantage. Raised planters are also ideal for the elderly or wheelchair bound, or for those who suffer with bad backs, since they remove much of the stooping necessary for many garden tasks.

Here, ingenious use has been made of old bricks to create a miniature garden in a raised border/bed. Tiny backyards can be transformed in this way, and container gardens demand very little effort to maintain once the design and ornament have been completed.

Retaining walls/Raised beds/Planters

Planning retaining walls

The most important aspect of a retaining wall for a raised bed or terrace is its strength, for even a relatively low terrace can put a very high loading on the wall. Indeed, for walls above 1.2m (4ft), you would be wise to seek expert advice from a structural engineer or a surveyor – and check with your local planning authority or building department, as they may insist on your taking measures to ensure the wall's stability.

Efficient drainage is also essential. If water cannot drain freely through the wall in very wet weather, the build-up of extra weight behind the wall caused by the trapped water may be enough to make it collapse. Therefore, regardless of the type of wall you want to build, you must pay a lot of attention to these two points.

Most types of walling material are suitable for constructing retaining walls – bricks, concrete or reconstituted stone walling blocks or natural stone. For heavy-duty walls, you can use pre-cast hollow concrete blocks, reinforced with steel rods and filled with concrete, which can be faced with a non-structural wall of brick, for example, or rendered with cement mortar for a smooth finish that can be painted. Even wood can be used for low retaining walls, provided heavy sections are used and they are well secured. Choose the material that will best fit in with the style of your garden,

whether it be formal or informal.

On sloping ground you should also decide how many terraces you are going to construct. As a rule, it is better to break up a slope into several shallow terraces rather than one or two very deep ones. Not only does this look better, but it is also safer since your retaining walls will not be under such great pressure. Also, very deep terraces will require much more excavation than shallow ones, so you will save yourself a lot of back-breaking work by opting for the latter.

(Above) Retaining walls are ideal for providing a distinct division between different levels of the garden. This split stone wall contains a raised bed and is gradually being submerged by the trailing plants above. The relative informality of the split stone produces an interesting contrast with the more formal appearance of the paving and lawn that surrounds it.
(Below) An unusual sloping raised bed provides a variation in level where none existed before. The retaining wall is of split stone, angled inwards and carefully constructed to maintain the shape and taper of the bed.

A planter of weathered stone with stone coping/capping fits perfectly with this neatly laid out, rather formal garden. Wide coping/capping stones provide a useful working surface as well as informal seating.

While you are digging the foundation and constructing the wall itself, excavate the ground behind to a shallow slope to prevent it from sliding forward and undoing all your hard work. The soil should be retained temporarily by wooden shuttering made from plywood sheets secured by stakes and wooden battens. The soil can be backfilled once the wall has been built and the mortar has cured.

Building the wall

Retaining walls up to 1.2m (4ft) in height should be at least 225mm (9in) thick for strength. Walls above 1.2m (4ft) high should be at least 300mm (12in) thick. If this means constructing two leaves of masonry, a bond should be selected that ties the two together (see pages 12–17).

Construct the wall in the normal manner, using cords and profile boards to mark its position and building up several courses at each end before filling in the gap in between.

At the top of the wall, you can add coping/cap stones which can double as informal seating if the wall borders a patio, or as a surface for arranging flower pots. If bricks are being used, a course of these laid on edge can be substituted for the coping/cap stones. However, in this particular case, a damp-proof course of bituminous felt or slates should be laid immediately underneath them to prevent damp from penetrating the wall from above.

Where hollow concrete blocks are to be used for the wall, L-shaped steel reinforcing rods should be set in the concrete foundations when they are poured and the blocks dropped over them as they are laid. The rods should be the same height as the finished wall. Once the wall has been built to its finished height, the hollow blocks should be filled completely with concrete of a very wet, "soupy" consistency to provide extra strength. Work the concrete down well with a stout piece of wood to prevent any cavities forming in it.

While it is possible to build a dry stone retaining wall, this does require considerable skill to provide the neces-

The foundation

A sound foundation is essential for a retaining wall since it must spread the load being applied to the rear face of the wall through the ground below.

All masonry retaining walls should have solid concrete strip foundations 150–200mm (6–8in) thick and three times the width of the wall laid in a trench about 500mm (1ft 8in) deep. For added stability, the foundation can be given a "key" by making the portion of the foundation in front of the wall deeper than the rest.

(Left) The ground level in this garden rose steeply from the house, so a brick retaining wall was built to provide a division between a small patio and the rest of the garden. An additional wall was added across the end of the patio to produce a flower bed.
(Above) As with all walls, a retaining wall needs a sound foundation and this begins with a well compacted layer of hardcore, followed by a layer of concrete.

sary strength, and is probably not something that should be attempted by an amateur. However, you can build one that is held together with mortar, using much the same methods as for any other wall using regular-shaped masonry such as bricks.

Select the stones carefully to provide a good bond, building the wall as two leaves with large stones laid across the leaves at regular intervals to tie them together. Ideally, these should project beyond the back of the wall and into the ground behind to provide added stability.

Unlike a freestanding stone wall, only one face (the exposed front one) should be built to a batter (that is, sloping inward); the rear face should be vertical, so a pair of modified batter frames will be necessary, each with one vertical upright and one sloping batten (see page 18).

The wall should be left for about a week for the mortar to harden before backfilling the soil behind it.

Reinforcing the wall

Tall walls and those built on light crumbly soil will need extra reinforcement. The former should have piers at each end and along its length at regular intervals. These should be incorporated in the bonding pattern where possible, or built alongside the wall and tied into it with wall ties or expanded metal mesh laid in the mortar joints.

Another way of reinforcing the wall is to build the base wider than the top and stagger the courses of the rear face so that the front remains vertical.

To provide stability, hooked steel rods can be bedded in the mortar joints and led back into the ground behind the wall where they are set in blocks of concrete.

Expansion joints will also be needed in long walls to allow for the movement of the masonry brought about by extremes of temperature. These are achieved by leaving vertical joints the height of the wall free of mortar. Instead, they should be packed with a flexible exterior-grade sealant. Expansion joints should be spaced at 3.6m (12ft) intervals in temperate regions. In areas that suffer extremes of summer and winter temperatures, they should be placed considerably closer together.

Providing drainage

It is essential to prevent a build-up of water behind the retaining wall, so you must take steps to incorporate some form of drainage into the wall in stages as you build it.

To allow water to drain through the wall you can either set lengths of 75mm (3in) clay or plastic pipe into the wall near its base with a fall/pitch toward the face, or you can leave some of the vertical joints between the bricks of the lowest course free of mortar. If you are building a wall of two leaves of masonry, it may be necessary to remove part of a brick in the rear course to provide a drainage route to the open joint in the front leaf. This opening in the rear of the wall should be packed with stone chippings or pieces of broken flower pot to prevent it from becoming clogged with silt. The drainage points should be added at 900mm (3ft) intervals along the wall.

Additional drainage can be provided by laying agricultural drainpipes along the foot of the wall at the rear, bedding them on coarse gravel and surrounding them with the same material. These pipes simply butt together and will allow the water to seep in before carrying it to the sides of the wall, where it can be directed to soakaways/dry wells.

Ideally, the wall should also be protected from penetrating damp which could damage the masonry. One way is to paint the rear face with two or three

The bricks are laid in the normal manner, building up a double-leaf wall for strength. Check that they are level and leave some of the joints in the bottom course free of mortar to provide "weep" holes for drainage. Alternatively, lengths of plastic or clay pipe can be bedded through the wall between the bricks.

Pin a line in place to act as a guide for building up the wall – construct the ends first and then fill in the gap between them. Check all the time that the individual brick courses are level and that the faces of the wall are truly vertical. In this situation, the new brickwork could be "toothed" into the existing wall, or long nails bedded into the mortar joints as ties.

A course of bricks laid on edge will act as coping/capping to the wall, but long paving stones can work equally well. When the wall is finished, point the mortar joints to finish them neatly and when the mortar has dried paint the inside of the retaining walls with bituminous sealant to prevent moisture from soaking into the bricks. When this has cured the soil and plants can be added.

coats of a bituminous sealer such as that used for damp-proofing floors. Another is to lay a thick plastic sheet up against its rear face after you have backfilled the ground to above the level of the drainage points.

Wooden retaining walls
Heavy logs and thick sections of wood such as old railway sleepers/railroad ties can also be used to build retaining walls, although care must be taken to ensure that they are securely fixed. Probably the simplest way of doing this is to drive 75–100mm (3–4in) section stakes into the ground at approximately 1.2m (4ft) intervals, making sure they go in at least 600mm (2ft). Or better still, set them in concrete as you would normal fence posts (see page 28).

Then lay the logs or sleepers/ties one on top of the other behind the stakes, packing a layer of hardcore or rubble behind them as you go, so that water will drain away from the wall rapidly. Stagger the sections of wood so that you don't produce continuous vertical joints.

For low walls, it is also possible to set the lengths of wood vertically in the ground, but they should be supported by horizontal cross-pieces nailed across the back of the sections, with struts being

Dry stone retaining walls, their joints packed with soil, are ideal for an informal cottage-style garden. They provide a good backdrop for colourful trailing plants that are allowed to spill down from the raised beds and that are planted between the stones. Crazy paving with moss and ground-cover plants growing between the stones completes a delightful, rambling corner of a much larger garden.

This colourfully planted raised bed with brick retaining walls provides an attractive break between the patio and the rest of the garden.

marking the edge of a patio. However, it should not be so high that some of its plants will be obscured, nor so wide as to make it impossible to reach across it – particularly if it can only be reached from one side. By the same token, it should not be so narrow that plants will quickly exhaust the goodness of the soil.

As a guide, raised planters should not be more than about 800mm (2ft 8in) high, and if only accessible from one side, no more than 500mm (1ft 8in) wide.

Weep holes or drainpipes should be set in the lowest courses of the planter, and its interior should be treated with bituminous sealer to prevent damp from penetrating the walls. The tops of the walls should have coping/cap stones or bricks laid on edge with a damp-proof course below. By lining the walls inside with slabs of 25–50mm (1–2in) thick polystyrene, you prevent the soil in the planter from freezing in winter, which would tend to push the walls outward.

taken back into the ground for reinforcement.

Needless to say, all the wood used for a retaining wall must be well treated with preservative, and preferably pressure treated. Where possible, a hardwood should be chosen.

Planters

Although planters still need retaining walls to contain the soil in them, the foundations need not be quite so strong, since there will not be a lot of soil to contain. It is often possible to construct a planter directly on top of the paved surface of a patio. However, where there isn't an existing hard-surfaced base on which to build the planter, you should construct concrete strip foundations as usual (see page 12). In fact, strip foundations are preferable since they allow the planter to drain more freely to the ground below and to draw moisture from it in times of low rainfall.

The size of the planter will depend on its position and whether it is to serve some other purpose as well – such as screening some aspect of the garden, providing seating around its edges or

Logs can be attractively used to construct retaining walls. A low log wall can be secured by stakes driven into the ground. Make sure all the wood is treated well with preservative, particularly the stakes, paying close attention to the endgrain.

Lumber makes a good material for retaining walls. Here railway sleepers/railroad ties have been stacked on top of each other to construct a low wall separating a raised bed from a gravel driveway. They have been laid slightly overlapping to provide a form of bond and, by careful cutting of the ends, the wall has been made to follow the curve of the driveway quite closely. When large sections of lumber are used in this way, they should be secured by driving steel rods down through holes drilled in them and into the ground, or by fixing them to stakes driven into the ground behind the wall.

Lay out the lowest course of logs so that you can decide on their exact position and then drive the stakes into the ground close to the end of each log. Continue to drive the stakes in until their tops are level with the desired finished height of the wall.

Add the logs, fixing them to the stakes with galvanized nails. Try to arrange the logs so that the ends of the second course are staggered in relation to the first course to provide a bond for extra strength. Fill in behind the logs with gravel to ensure good drainage before adding the soil.

SEATS AND BARBECUES

A garden should be a place where you and your family can relax and enjoy being outdoors whenever the weather permits. So after you have laid it out and planted it, you should make some provision for using the garden. And an important use is being able to sit in it in peace – to read a book or follow some other pastime, or just to take in its sights, sounds, and scents.

There is a vast range of ready-made garden furniture to choose from, ranging from simple wooden seats to well-upholstered loungers with sun canopies, but often a seat that is tailored to blend in with its surroundings looks best. This usually means making one yourself, using materials that complement the style of the garden.

Designing seats is a complex business, but provided you take care to keep your structures simple and sturdy you should have no problems. They can be built completely from wood, from a combination of wood and masonry, or from masonry only, using basic skills.

A natural progression from just sitting in the garden on a fine day is to dine in it too and if you want to dine, why not cook as well? If you are really serious, a built-in barbecue is the answer. This can be as simple or as complex as you wish, and may be combined with seating or, perhaps, a raised planter containing herbs which will always be at hand for cooking.

Professional joinery skills would be needed to make a bench such as this one; but the idea of constructing a roof over a dead tree trunk with, perhaps, a more simply constructed shady seat below gives rise to some interesting possibilities for the average do-it-yourselfer.

Wooden seats and benches

(**Above**) A weathered garden chair in a quiet corner of the garden is an invitation to relax.

(**Above**) A longer seat allows you to share the tranquil pleasures of the garden with others. Left to its own devices, wood will weather to a delightful silver-gray colour that will be in total harmony with the surrounding foliage. This seat stands on small tiles set into the lawn. These not only protect the legs from rising damp but also allow the seat to be set level.

(**Right**) A seat built round a tree will provide a shady spot in which to sit, and the method of construction is quite simple. Remember to allow growing room for the tree trunk.

Making wooden seats

Wood is often chosen for making garden furniture because not only is it easy to work with but, being a natural material, it blends in well with the garden setting. Choosing wood for outdoor use needs careful thought, however, particularly if the furniture is to be left outside all year round.

The softwoods that are commonly available will soon begin to rot if left exposed to the elements without some form of protection, and this means treating them with liberal applications of preservative or, better still, buying the timber already pressure-treated with preservative. However, softwoods are relatively inexpensive and provided the sections are thick enough to provide sufficient strength they can be used for garden furniture.

Better still would be to use a wood with a natural resistance to weather such as western red cedar, teak or iroko.

You can construct a bath for soaking wood in preservative from simple materials. First, arrange a surround of bricks on the ground, making sure they are roughly level.

Next, lay a thick plastic sheet in the centre of the bricks, folding its edges at the corners so that it fits snugly inside. Take care not to disturb any of the bricks.

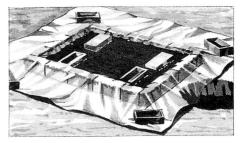

Place bricks around the outside of the plastic to trap its edges and then fill the centre with preservative. Lay the wood in place and weight it down to soak.

When you have finished with the bath, sink a bucket in the ground next to it, remove a brick and allow the preservative to flow into the bucket.

However, these woods may not be quite so easy to find and they will be more expensive.

Buy your wood ready-planed and examine it carefully for twists, warps, splits and knots – all of which are undesirable. It is always best to explain to your supplier just what you want it for so that he can sort out the best pieces. Take your time in finding and selecting the wood – remember, you will want it to last a long time in a potentially harsh environment.

You can provide protection for wooden outdoor furniture by treating it with a yacht varnish or lacquer; however, this needs applying every year to retain the protective finish and very soon this becomes a tedious chore. In addition, this treatment tends to give the wood a slightly unnatural look which might be out of place in many gardens.

All good-quality ready-made garden furniture will have been assembled with glued and dowelled joints. The various wooden sections will have been cut to fit together to ensure strong connections without the need for screws or nails. However, unless you already have some experience in carpentry and possess the necessary woodworking tools, you will be unable to use this method of assembly

(Above) This ornate seat is perfect for a more formal garden and provides added visual interest. Not easy to construct, unless you have plenty of experience in carpentry, but very attractive in the right setting.

Wooden seats and benches

in your own garden furniture. Consequently you will have to rely on overlapping the various pieces and securing them with screws and glue. There is nothing wrong with this, provided you take care – indeed much of the cheaper ready-made garden furniture is made in this way.

When choosing screws for garden furniture, make sure they are brass or stainless steel. Ordinary steel screws – even if they have been treated with protective lacquer or have been chromium plated – will rust, not only causing streaks and stains on the wood but also becoming weak in the process. When using brass screws, particularly thin ones, be careful when driving them in, since the greater the force required to turn them the more likely they are to snap off. It is always better to drive a steel screw of the same size in first to cut a thread in the wood and then fit in the brass screw. Countersink all the screw heads so that they won't snag on clothing.

For added strength, all joints should be glued, but make sure you use a suitable exterior-quality wood glue – many types will deteriorate when exposed to damp conditions, weakening your furniture.

Methods of construction

Any garden seat must be soundly made and strong enough to take the weight of the person – or persons – sitting on it. For a start, this means using substantial sections of wood, particularly if working with a softwood. For a garden seat, the part you sit on should be slatted to allow rainwater to drain off, and the slats should be 32–38mm (1¼–1½in) thick. They can vary in width, depending on the type of seat you are making. A couple of 175mm (7in) wide boards with a 13mm (½in) gap in between would do for a simple seat, or you could use several 75mm (3in) wide slats instead. The same material could be used to produce a slatted back.

The seat needs a simple supporting framework and it would be best to use something like 75 × 50mm (4 × 2in) sections for this. The framework would comprise sets of legs joined by two cross-pieces – one at the top to provide a support for the seat slats, and one near the feet to prevent the legs from splaying out. In addition, the seat would need long rails running the length of the seat to prevent the legs from splaying sideways. These should be fixed near the feet as well.

If the seat is to have a back, the rear

(*Above*) There is nothing like making the most of materials you have on hand in the garden, and a seat of this type could not be much simpler. Two tree stumps have been cut to form L-shapes and then boards nailed between them. Only do this if you have to fell the trees, or if they have already been felled – it would be criminal to cut down trees simply to make a seat.

(*Right*) What do you do with the felled trees? Well, apart from cutting them up for firewood, if the trunks are thick enough how about seats? Although it looks quite simple, a seat like this requires some skilled use of a chainsaw.

Wooden seats and benches

(Left) For a less formal garden, rustic poles can be used to construct a seat. Careful thought must be given to bracing the structure, as the pieces are simply overlapped and nailed together. This tends to make it look rather heavy, but it is effective nonetheless.

(Below) A very attractive semi-circular seat at Misarden Park in Gloucestershire, England. The white paint makes it stand out starkly against the backdrop of the stone wall.

legs can be extended upward to provide a fixing for the back slats.

With this type of construction, all the various pieces are joined by simply overlapping them. Each joint is glued and reinforced by two screws that are long enough to pass through one piece and halfway through its mate.

One problem with any construction of this kind is that with use the bench may fold sideways, but this can be prevented by adding one or two diagonal braces between the leg frames or across the back.

The slatted construction can be used in many ways, and there are various permutations of leg frame – for example, the legs may be perfectly vertical or set at an angle. Sections of seat built in this way could even be joined together to form a seat around a tree.

(Above) Seats are more interesting when they are designed to fit their surroundings. This long L-shaped seat fits neatly into a corner and provides both somewhere to sit and visual interest to what would otherwise be a boring view.

(Below) Seats can often be incorporated in walls and other structures. Here, a simple board is placed between very stout walls that look as though originally they had some

other purpose. Notice how the wood weathers to a colour that blends perfectly with the colour of the stones.

(Above right) Trees make ideal spots for sitting and, if you want to enjoy the shade for a short break, this simple bench is the answer, with its two concrete supporting pillars and a thick wooden board placed between them.

The dimensions of the seat can vary depending on its position and how many people you expect will use it at one time, although its overall size should not be such that it overwhelms the garden. For a simple two-seater, make it 1.2–1.5m (4–5ft) long, and for this size you would need three leg frames – one at each end and one in the middle. The height of the seat slats should be about 425–450mm (17–18in) from the ground.

The seat should be built initially on a level surface so that you can ensure that all the legs are the same length and the seat will not rock to and fro. If the legs are of unequal length, they can be marked for cutting by standing the seat on a level surface, propping it so that the seat base is level and then marking round the base of each leg with a pencil held on top of a small block of wood.

If the seat is to stand on a lawn, however, you may find that it will still rock because the lawn itself is not perfectly level. In this case, you can pack pieces of slate or tile beneath the feet until it stands firmly. Indeed, placing pieces of tile or slate beneath the feet is a wise precaution to prevent moisture from being drawn up into the endgrain of the legs.

Another method of building wooden

Stone seats and benches

Stone can be used to good effect for seating, although you may have to buy seats ready-made in this material.
(**Above**) Ornate stone supports actually carry wooden seats which are shaped to match the curve of the wall behind.
(**Above right**) Using flat sections of stone, you can build a seat into a wall.
(**Above, far right**) A simple stone bench provides a convenient spot to stop and sit a while on a stroll through the garden. You may find such seats through architectural salvage companies.
(**Right**) Don't neglect a seat in a wall, otherwise you may find it taken over by other inhabitants of the garden.

seats, which is ideal for a patio, is to construct planked boxes, using tongued-and-grooved boards with slatted tops. The boards should be joined at the corners by sections of 100 × 50mm/ 4 × 2in wood which will project about 50mm (2in) below the lowest board to form feet. Additional supports should be added for long boxes and crosspieces fixed to support the top. The tops can be removable, allowing the boxes to double as storage containers if you install a bottom panel inside, and the construction can also be extended to form planters.

Masonry seats

Bricks and blocks can also be used in the construction of garden seats. A simple double-leaf wall topped with concrete slabs can serve as an occasional seat, and a flight of steps can be extended sideways for form seating for a patio. Similarly, raised planters can be decked at one end with slabs for sitting on.

Alternatively, masonry can be neatly combined with wood to make seats. In its simplest form, two brick or block pedestals could be built and a simple slatted wooden seat base dropped over their tops. For something more ambitious, a curving wall could be constructed with projecting piers to support a slatted wooden seat base. Or piers could be added to an existing wall for a seat.

What can you buy?

There is no doubt that making your own garden furniture can be a very rewarding activity, allowing you to tailor seats and benches to fit their surroundings. However, unless you are skilled in carpentry, such work is likely to be difficult and time consuming, and while ready-made garden furniture is expensive, the quality of finish and the range available makes it well worth considering.

You can buy anything from a simple bench to an ornate seat in styles that range from the classic patterns of yesteryear to the most modern designs in both wood and metal.

Barbecues

Siting the barbecue

Deciding where you are going to put a barbecue requires some thought. Obviously, you won't want it too far from the house (especially a long walk from the kitchen) – and don't forget you might have to make a dash for cover if the weather turns sour. On the other hand, you won't want it immediately under a window or near a door, otherwise you may fill the house with smoke. Similarly, you won't be too popular with your neighbours if the smoke billows in their direction. Keep your barbecue away from trees and bushes too, as the intense heat given off may damage them, or even cause them to catch fire.

You may want to construct a barbecue as part of a patio, linking it with seating and/or planters and, if you wish, you can make it quite a complex structure with work surfaces, shelves and storage cupboards.

Types of barbecue

Basically, you have two choices with regard to the type of barbecue you construct. You may want a simple screened surface on which to stand a small ready-made barbecue, or you might prefer to construct one that incorporates its own firebed and grill. The latter requires a bit more work, but will provide you with a much larger barbecue that will extend the range of your outdoor cookery. You can buy prefabricated kits containing all the necessary metal pieces for this sort of barbecue, or you can assemble one yourself, using a grill from an old cooker and a large roasting pan as a firebed.

Probably the simplest type of built-in barbecue comprises a U-shaped brick or block wall with 10mm/½in steel pipe or cast iron supports set in the mortar joints for the metal firebed and grill. Two or three sets of grill supports should be added to allow the grill to be lifted or lowered in relation to the firebed to suit the food being cooked, and a few holes punched in the bottom of

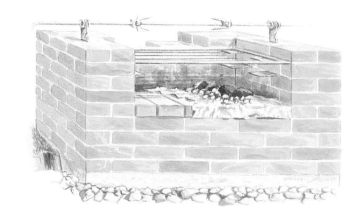

A barbecue can be as simple or as complex as you wish, depending on how you intend to use it. The simplest construction takes the form of a U-shaped brick surround with a firebed and supports for the grill built in. As with all brick structures it should be built on a foundation of concrete laid over a hardcore base. The surround can be built as a simple box up to the level of the firebed and filled with hardcore. Proper firebricks should be used for the firebed itself and its surrounds, *those of the bed being laid loose and wrapped in aluminum foil. The sides and back of the box should then be built up by several more courses to provide a wind-shield and support for the grill and any other fittings you may incorporate, such as a spit. Build two or three sets of grill supports into the brickwork so that you can adjust the grill's height to suit the food you are cooking.*

A well-organized barbecue corner with plenty of work surface and a chimney to funnel smoke away.

the firebed to allow an updraft to ensure efficient burning of the charcoal.

The wall should be continued above the topmost grill position to provide a windshield.

An alternative to this construction would be to build the lower portion of the structure as a box, filling it with rubble, and laying firebricks across the top on a bed of sand. These would then provide a firebed for the charcoal. They should not be held with mortar, but left loose so that they can expand with the heat from the barbecue. If you just want a surface on which to stand a ready-made barbecue, use ordinary bricks instead of firebricks and set them in place with mortar.

The basic U-shaped wall can be extended in several ways to provide extra supports for wooden shelving or to form a work surface topped with marble or concrete slabs.

(Above) Barbecues can be freestanding or built into a wall surrounding a patio. This one is a good size with plenty of work surface around it and handy recesses for storing fuel and other barbecue necessities. *(Right)* For a blazing log fire outdoors, this curved windshield is ideal.

WATER FEATURES

Whether it be a formal, regularly shaped pond set in the middle of a paved patio or an informal, irregularly shaped pool at the foot of a rock garden, water adds another dimension of enjoyment to your garden. A still sheet of water gives a peaceful air to the garden and provides mirror images of the surroundings and the changing sky, whereas moving water provides sound and varying patterns and colours as sunlight plays upon it.

It is a lucky garden owner who has a natural stream or spring just waiting there to be landscaped into pools and falls. Most of us have to start from scratch. Today, however, it is made much easier for us, and the range of equipment and ready-made accessories is continually increasing for the new pond owner. Electrical pumps, filtering tanks, underwater lighting and a wide variety of styles and designs of fountains are easy to find.

Waterfalls and fountains can be added to ponds to provide extra interest, and a variety of water plants and fish can make them quite fascinating features in their own right.

At one time constructing a pond was a complicated business, relying on a concrete lining to contain the water. This often failed because of cracks that developed as a result of ground movement. Now, however, construction is much simpler, thanks to the availability of ready-made rigid fiberglass liners and flexible butyl rubber liners.

Weathered stone predominates in this corner of a garden where a large oblong pool has been established for some years. The gentle trickle of water from a basin fountain with its elegant statuette adds another dimension to an already idyllic design. Although a pool of this size is beyond the scope of most of us, a smaller adaptation is perfectly feasible.

Ponds

Siting your pond

Once you decide that you want to add a pond to your garden, your most important decision will be where to put it, which will depend on several factors. First, what sort of pond will it be? A formal rectangular or round pond will probably look best as the central feature of a paved patio rather than placed in the middle of a lawn; whereas an informal, natural-looking pond should be at the lowest point of your garden, since water always drains toward a low point.

A pond should receive plenty of daylight, so don't put it where it is in constant shade, and don't put it under deciduous trees if you intend to keep fish in it. The falling leaves will sink to the bottom and decompose, giving off a poison that will kill fish. If you have no option but to put it near trees, then stretch fine netting over it to catch the leaves in the autumn.

Although a pond should receive plenty of light, direct sunlight will encourage the growth of algae which will turn the water to "pea soup." However, you can counteract this by adding water plants which consume the nutrients in the water that the algae feed on and which will shade the surface of the water. Water snails can also be introduced to eat algae.

Another consideration is whether you want to install a pump for a waterfall or fountain since this will require running an electrical cable to the house; it is best if you can keep such cable runs to a minimum.

The pond should be on level ground, but if your garden slopes you can overcome this by digging away the ground on the up-slope side and holding it back with a retaining wall (built as part of a rockery if you want a natural look), and building up the down-slope side with more soil and possibly another retaining wall (see page 60).

Ponds and children

Safety is another consideration if you have young children, or there are young children in the neighbourhood. Inevitably, they will be fascinated by the water and may need constant supervision when in the garden – even a shallow pond will contain sufficient water to drown a small child. It may be better to build a raised pond in this case, or to find some means of restricting children to the part of the garden that does not contain the pond.

Pets and even wild animals that use the garden may also be at risk, particularly if the pond has an overhanging rim that makes it impossible for them to

(Right) This rather formal pond has been brightened up considerably by extensive planting in and around it which relaxes its structured appearance. The use of paving slabs as stepping stones is an effective way of providing access to the rest of the garden and allows the pond to be much wider than would otherwise be possible.

(Below left) A semi-formal approach has been adopted here, the ordered appearance of the brick retaining wall contrasting strongly with the stone walls at the back of the pond. Again, extensive planting contributes to an attractive setting.

(Below) Still in its early days, this pond has a more informal look provided by its irregular shape and the stone walls surrounding it. Care should be exercised when siting a pond near trees – raking dead leaves off in autumn can be a chore, and if left to rot they will poison fish.

Ponds

(**Above**) This well-established circular pond fits in well with the rather formal appearance of the rest of the garden. Because it is set in the centre of a wide paved area, it could look quite uninteresting but for the statue which focuses the attention wonderfully.

(**Above right**) A well established pond can be a delight to the eye, particularly when surrounded by colourful plants. Fish, too, can provide great interest, and it can be very relaxing just to watch them feeding near the surface. If you keep fish make sure the pond is wide enough and deep enough to discourage cats from attempting to catch them. The raised planter behind this pond gives depth to the setting, creating an attractive corner of the garden.

(**Right**) Even a simple rectangular pond can be very effective if treated in the right manner. The brick edging here links the pond to the patio, which is paved in the same material, making it part of an integrated design, rather than looking like an afterthought. Brightly coloured plants around the pond make for an attractive setting, reinforced by the splashes of colour from the water lilies. Movement and the gentle sound of running water are provided by the ornate basin from which water is allowed to trickle into the pond.

climb out should they fall in. This can be overcome by preparing a shallow "beach" of pebbles in a more natural-looking pool; but in a formal edged pond, probably the easiest solution is to place bricks or blocks near the edge just below the surface to form steps.

Types of pond liner

You have two basic choices when it comes to buying a pond liner: rigid or flexible. The rigid liner is made from fiberglass and is available in a fairly wide range of shapes and sizes. These liners are very tough and virtually leakproof. However, you are still limited to the manufacturer's idea of what is the ideal shape and size, and often they are made in very pale colours that will take quite some time to tone down and "disappear."

Semi-rigid liners in vacuum-formed plastic are also available, but although they are cheaper than the rigid types, they are nowhere near as strong, and you would probably be better off using a flexible liner.

Flexible liners may be made from PVC reinforced with nylon or from butyl rubber. Of the two, the rubber version is the strongest and will often be guaranteed for 20 years, although it may last much longer than that – perhaps as long as 50 years.

With a flexible liner, you have much more choice when it comes to the shape of your pond since the material will stretch or fold to match practically any shape you care to mention. The weight of the water will make it hold its shape, the top edges being retained by paving slabs or natural stone.

A flexible pond liner is supplied as a flat sheet, and all you have to do is add twice the depth of the pond to its width and to its length to obtain the dimensions of the sheet you require. If your dimensions don't quite match those of a standard size sheet, simply buy the next size up.

Installing a rigid liner

When making a pond with a rigid fiberglass liner, you must take care to dig out the hole so that it matches the shape of the liner as closely as possible. This will ensure that it is adequately supported all around. Because all but the simplest of rigid liners will have not only a tapering shape toward the bottom but also planting steps and both shallow and deep areas, this is not so easy.

One way in which it can be done is to set the liner on the ground so that its rim is horizontal. Then mark around the lowest section of the liner with some form of scriber. Remove the pond and dig a hole to slightly outside the marked lines down to the depth of the bottom section of the liner. Then drop the liner back into place and mark out the next section on the ground. Dig this out as before, at the same time digging out the inner hole for the lower section of the liner. Continue in this way until you have reproduced the shape of the liner in the ground.

Open up the hole by about 38mm (1½in) all round, and dig each layer lower by the same amount, sloping the sides at about 60 degrees to match the sides of the liner. Then add a 38mm (1½in) layer of damp sand to the sides, shelves and bottom of the hole. Lower the liner into place, shaking it to bed it completely, packing in more sand around the edges if necessary.

Fill the liner with water to within about 50mm (2in) of the rim and then conceal the rim by bedding paving stones or rocks on pads of mortar around the edge. The edging stones should overhang the rim by about 50mm (2in).

Installing a flexible liner

With a flexible liner, mark out the shape of your pond on the ground using thick rope or garden hose pipe for curved lines. There is no need to dig your pond to any great depth – 450 to 500mm (18 to 24in) being sufficient – although, if you want to keep fish, you should stick to the deeper figure.

Dig out the shape of the pond, remembering to slope the sides at about 60 degrees and to leave shelves at the sides for planting water plants. These should be 225mm (9in) wide and 225mm (9in)

Ponds

(Above) Flexible rubber pond liners are very versatile and can be worked into virtually any shape. Begin work on your pond by marking out its shape on the ground. A garden hose is ideal for this as it forms natural curves. For a rectangular pond mark it out using pegs and cords.

(Above) Having marked out the shape of the pond, begin digging it out to the required depth. Carefully remove any turf at the edges to provide a ledge for the stones that will conceal and retain the edges of the liner. If you plan to use water plants, incorporate additional ledges a good 225mm (9in) below the intended water level.

(Above) You must ensure that the ledge surrounding the pond is level, otherwise the water level will be close to the edging stones on one side and way below them at another. Check by resting a long, straight piece of wood and a builder's level across the ledges. If necessary, remove extra soil until the edge is level all round.

below the final water level. Take care to remove all sharp stones from the sides and bottom of the hole, otherwise they may puncture the flexible liner.

Again, the excavation should be lined with a layer of damp sand or damp newspapers, if you prefer.

Lay the liner out over the hole, making sure it overlaps by an equal amount at each side, and then place bricks or stones all around to hold it in place. Run a hose into the middle of the liner and begin to fill it with water. The weight of the water will gradually pull the liner into the shape of the hole, although you may have to put a few pleats and folds into it to make it fit snugly.

Once the water has reached to within 50mm (2in) of the rim, trim off any surplus liner and add edging stones as described for the rigid liner. These will

(Above) Continue filling the pond – which will take some time for even a relatively small one – shaping and folding the liner as you go to fit it into all the recesses of the hole. Turn off the water when its level is about 50mm (2in) below the ledge around the pond.

(Above) Once the pond has been filled with water, trim the edges of the liner so that it fits neatly into the ledge cut for the retaining stones. Never cut sections from the liner to make it fold more easily, as this could lead to the development of tears and leaks.

(*Above*) *It is important to protect the liner from punctures caused by stones in the soil beneath the pond. Go over the excavated site carefully, removing all the stones you can find. Then add a layer of damp sand to the bottom of the hole. Alternatively, you can use damp newspapers, which can readily be formed to the shape of the hole.*

(*Above*) *Continue adding sand, extending the layer up the sides of the hole until the entire excavation is covered. Smooth it off carefully with your hand and make one final check for any stones that you may have carried in on your boots. When you are satisfied, you can add the liner.*

(*Above*) *Arrange the liner over the hole so that it overlaps it evenly on all sides, then roughly form it into shape by hand. Place bricks or stones around the liner edges to hold them down and begin to fill the pond with a hose. As the weight of water increases, the rubber will stretch exactly to the pond's shape.*

(*Above*) *Any flat stones can be used to edge the pond and conceal the liner. Bed them on mortar and make sure they overhang the edge of the pond by about 50mm (2in). That way, they will conceal the liner exposed above water level. In this instance, broken stones have been used to give a crazy paving effect.*

(*Above*) *Fit the stones together carefully, making sure they are set level and bedded securely. Here, the joints are being finished by raking out with a screwdriver. You could, however, leave the mortar flush with the surface of the stones.*

not only conceal the liner above water level, but will also protect it from exposure to direct sunlight which may damage it.

A flexible liner can also be used for constructing a pool with raised edges. Simply build low walls from brick or block on concrete strip foundations, making them wide enough to accept concrete slabs as coping/cap stones. Make sure the ground inside the wall is free of sharp stones, then add the liner, bedding its edges in the mortar joints beneath the coping/cap stones.

If required, ledges for water plants can be formed around the edge of a raised pool by digging out the ground in the centre and sloping the sides as you would for a sunken pond. The coping/cap stones around the edge will also provide room for potted plants or seating.

Waterfalls

The sound of running water can be particularly restful, whether it is the gentle burble of a tumbling stream or the more insistent rush of a steep waterfall. Both can be incorporated into your pond scene and are especially attractive when combined with a rockery.

It is possible to buy rigid waterfall liners that comprise a series of small pools with lips that direct the water from an upper reservoir to the main pond. Installing one of these is a relatively straightforward operation, requiring a number of steps to be cut into the slope of your rockery and then the rigid liner to be bedded on them with sand. Rocks can then be placed around the edges to conceal the liner.

Unfortunately, because the water flowing down a rigid waterfall liner will be relatively shallow, the unnatural colour of the fiberglass will always be visible and will spoil the effect. A much better solution is to use pieces of flexible rubber liner to make a watercourse with a series of stepped pools feeding one into another.

Another advantage of using a flexible

liner, of course, is that you can tailor your waterfall to suit your own ideas. You might want water cascading down a series of steps and flowing along a short channel to the main pond. Or you might prefer to have it fall some distance from a small pool directly into the pond. Both can be arranged with careful digging, placing of the liner, and positioning of rocks and stones.

Basically you need to dig out the pools and watercourse, line them with sand and then add sections of flexible liner. The liner from an upper pool should be arranged to overlap that of the pool below, each being held in place and disguised by stones placed against it. Extra stones should be placed around the edges of the pools and across the lips where they discharge into the pool below. For the channel that feeds into the main pond, leave a section of liner in place when you trim off the excess, and dig a shallow trench for it to lie in.

The water for the waterfall is circulated by a submersible electric pump which usually takes its power from a transformer connected to the normal mains electricity supply. The transformer reduces the voltage to a level that will not injure anyone who should accidentally touch anything live. This is

Less dramatic, but equally pleasing, is this cleverly designed watercourse with very natural looking falls to a pond below.

particularly important whenever electricity is used near water since the two make a fatal combination.

Water is delivered to the top of the waterfall by a hose connected to the pump. This should be concealed underground alongside the waterfall with its open end concealed by a rock where it discharges into the reservoir at the top of the waterfall.

The power cable for the pump, which sits on the floor of the pond, should be run under one of the edging stones and then taken to a waterproof connector linking it with a cable to the transformer.

Although the low-voltage carried by the cable between pump and transformer will not give you a serious electric shock, you should take steps to protect the cable from accidental damage. Don't leave it lying on the ground where, if nothing else, it could trip someone up, and don't run it along a fence which might be blown over. By far the best idea is to run it through a plastic conduit underground. This will provide total protection.

(Above) A waterfall fits this rockery well.
(Left) A tall waterfall can be very impressive, but needs a lot of room.

Fountains

Another attractive water feature is the fountain which, like the waterfall, is operated by a submersible pump sitting on the floor of the pond, or on a platform of bricks or blocks if the pond is deep. Indeed, some pumps combine a fountain with a flexible hose outlet that can feed a waterfall as well.

The important thing is to choose a fountain that will not overpower the effect of your pond. It should not shoot its jets so high that wind-blown spray falls outside the pond. Nor should it be over-elaborate if the pond is small. Fountains are ideal for formal ponds but should not be included in those that are

supposed to look natural – the two just don't go together.

In most cases the fountain outlet simply projects above the pump and it can usually be fitted with a range of fountain heads that vary the pattern of the water jets. The pump should be positioned so that the head just projects

A fountain is one way of providing added interest to a more formal pond. Fountains come in many forms, from simple to grand. (Above) An ornate basin with a central fountain can make a fine centrepiece for a large pond, or it could be allowed to stand on its own as a focal point for a paved area. (Right) Mask fountains can also be used to good effect. Here the water flows into a small stone trough. The ledge provides a useful display point for potted plants and fossils, which can be seen through the narrow window.

above the level of the water in the pond.

In some cases, it is possible to connect floating fountain heads to the pump, and these may incorporate waterproof lights as well for use at night. Indeed, with either a waterfall or a fountain, it pays to consider the other uses you can make of the power supply to them. You can use the same low-voltage supply to operate garden lighting, which will give another pleasing aspect to your garden at night.

One point to remember with a fountain is that the wind will inevitably carry some of the water away, so after a prolonged dry spell you may need to top up the level of the water in the pond.

Although this pond has quite an informal appearance with its natural stone edging and cottage garden style planting, the fountain and statue are more likely to be found in a formal setting. However, they do provide considerable visual impact and help create a "busy" corner against a rather featureless backdrop.

Bridges

Bridges can be constructed in many forms, some of which are purely practical, while others may have a more decorative aspect. However, all should be solidly made and built on firm foundations.
(Left) A simple slatted wooden bridge works well in this setting, but its proximity to the fountain means that not only will the slats be wet and slippery but also anyone crossing the bridge may get soaked.
(Right) Stepping stones are a very effective method of continuing a path across a pond. The apparently haphazard way in which these are arranged makes them look as though they have always been there.
(Far right) A bridge of rustic poles can be simply made and looks perfect for this very natural-looking garden. Handrails are a sensible safety feature.
(Below right) Using the same paving for a bridge as the path it connects gives a unified appearance.

A bridge makes an attractive addition to any water feature in your garden, allowing you to integrate the feature fully into the garden design and permitting a path to take a logical route rather than being forced to skirt the pond or "stream." Similarly, the inclusion of a bridge in your path will allow the provision of a much larger pond than might otherwise be possible.

You can construct a bridge in many different styles to suit the tone of your garden and the style of your water feature. In its simplest form it may comprise two stout pieces of wood anchored to the ground and decked with boards or slats. However, for safety, you should add handrails, which are essential if children or the elderly use the garden.

Simple handrails can be supported by a vertical post at each end of the bridge or you may prefer an ornate balustrade along each side – you can use fittings from an interior staircase for this, provided the wood is treated well with preservative or painted.

It is important that your bridge is stoutly made, since the last thing you want is for it to collapse into the water when you walk across it. For the main supports use 150mm (6in) square wooden posts pressure-treated with preservative, decking them with 25mm (1in) thick boards secured by galvanized nails. Keep the span to no more than 1.2m (4ft), otherwise you may find that the bridge begins to sag after a while – if necessary, arrange the shape of the pond to allow this.

The main supports should be fixed to concrete foundations at each end with expansion bolts/shields. The foundations themselves should take the form of 150mm (6in) thick concrete footings set into the ground about 300mm (1ft) back from the edge of the pond and measuring 300mm (1ft) deep by the width of the path. Make sure the bridge supports are level before decking them – you can pack tiles or slates beneath the ends if necessary.

A bridge can also be simulated by constructing two ponds side by side with a narrow strip of ground between them. The bridge supports can then be laid directly on top of this after installing the pond liners and edging. By making the supports and decking overhang the edges of the ponds, you will create the appearance of a proper bridge. Wide paving slabs can also be used in the same way to create the appearance of a "floating" path.

ROCK GARDENS

The traditional rockery with its layers of large rocks and colourful alpine plants can make a very striking feature if executed properly. Resembling a rocky outcrop on a mountain or a cliff face, it is an ideal way to link the different levels of a garden. But rockeries are not always easy to build, and stones of the size needed to create the right effect are sometimes difficult to obtain and move. So think it all through carefully.

Rocks and stones have many uses in the garden, and with a little imagination the attractive qualities of gravel, stone chips, pebbles, and large weathered boulders can all be used in their own right to produce unusual eyecatching features.

Dry stream beds can be simulated, for example, or large, unusually shaped rocks can be treated like sculptures, and gravel can be laid to better effect than pocket-size lawns in small walled gardens. By combining many different types and textures of stone imaginatively, you can make a tranquil Japanese-style garden with very little actual planting.

A circular rock garden has been created as a focal point for this wall-enclosed corner. The bird bath with its statue furnish the highest point with symmetrical purpose, while the rocks are organized in a simple terrace construction that is easy to plant and maintain.

Rockeries

One of the most important features of a rockery is that it should look like a natural rocky outcrop rather than a heap of large stones with plants growing on it. This requires considerable skill in selecting the site and the stones, and laying the stones so they look as though they belong together. Very little soil should be visible in a rockery – it should be packed into crevices between and in the rocks and is even better if covered with a layer of gravel. This will not only disguise its presence but also helps to retain moisture during the summer.

Choosing the site

As with so many features in the garden it is vitally important to choose the correct site for a rockery. Don't forget that you are trying to reproduce a natural setting, so it really should not have a wall, a fence, or your house as a backdrop if avoidable. Ideally, a hedge or trees should be behind the rockery.

Although you can build a rockery on flat ground, it is much better if you can build it into the face of an existing slope in your garden. This should be a sunny position, although it should not be in full sun all day long. It should definitely not be in shade, nor should it be under trees which will drip rainwater on to your alpine plants.

The site and the rockery itself should be well drained and the foundations firm.

Choosing the stone

Wherever possible try to use local stone for your rockery as this will be most in keeping with the area, your garden and your home. This will also help keep down the transport costs which make up a considerable amount of the overall cost of the stone. If stone is not available locally, choose sandstone or limestone as these weather well into attractive shapes.

You should ask for a selection of sizes from your local stone merchant or mason's supplier, garden supplier or quarry, telling them that you want the material for a rockery. They may sell it by weight or size, and you will want a lot – several tons for a decent size rockery.

A rockery makes an attractive feature in any garden, but requires care in construction if it is to look right. The rocks must be large, arranged in natural-looking strata, and have little soil showing between them once planted.

This well established rockery shows how colourful they can be and how the rocks provide a rugged backdrop for the plants.

Bear in mind that you must get the rocks to your site, and that may not be easy. If you have access, you could rent a mechanical digger/backhoe and driver to shift the rock from your driveway (where it will be dumped on delivery) to the rockery's position. If there isn't access to the site for this type of equipment, you are in for a back-breaking task of moving the rock piece by piece.

One of the important things to watch is that you don't strain your back in attempting to move the rocks. Even apparently small pieces will be very heavy; if you are able to lift them, do so by bending your knees and keeping your back straight. There are various ways in which you can move the rocks over the ground. Smaller pieces can be moved by wheelbarrow, but larger rocks will need rolling along using stout wooden levers or crowbars. You may also be able to move them using wooden rollers on a track made of wooden planks laid on the ground. Rope slings can also be fashioned and fitted around rocks so that they can be lifted between two people.

Building the rock garden

Having selected a suitable site for the rockery, the first thing to do is outline its perimeter using pegs and cords. Then dig out the topsoil within the marked outline down to a depth of about 150mm (6in). Put the topsoil to one side, as you will use it later to help set the stones and provide a growing medium for the plants. Compact the subsoil well by treading it down or ramming it down with the end of a stout length of wood, such as a fence post.

Mix some of the topsoil with a loam-based compost and a little fine gravel and spread this in a 100mm (4in) layer across the foundation of the rockery. Then select the largest of your stones

Rockeries

(Above) A rockery in its early days can look quite bleak. This example shows how the rocks should be arranged in horizontal layers to resemble natural rock formations. Spreading gravel between the stones not only helps retain moisture in the soil but also maintains the appearance of a rocky outcrop.

(Below) Here, semi-dressed stones have been used to construct a form of rockery. Although they don't have the natural appearance of undressed stones, they do make quite an effective focal point for this bed. Stones of this type could be used to construct fake ruined walls as a backdrop for trailing plants.

and examine it from all sides to find the best aspect. This will become the keystone, which is set at the bottom and midpoint of the rockery, and all the others will be positioned from it. If the stone has strata, it should be laid so that these run at a slight downward angle toward the back of the slope, and all the other stones should be laid in the same way. Remember, the rocks were formed in horizontal layers under great pressure, so to resemble a natural outcrop of rock, the strata would still be roughly horizontal. Also, if the rock has a weathered face this should face outward.

Set the keystone in place, excavating some of the soil underneath so that it appears to be a small exposed portion of a much larger rock underneath. Then add more stones on each side in the same manner, working back from the keystone in a rough V-shape toward the back of the slope. All the rocks should be laid with a slight tilt toward the back of the slope so that rainwater will trickle back down their faces and into the soil below. Otherwise, the roots of the plants may not receive sufficient water for growth.

Make sure the rocks are firmly bedded and then backfill with more topsoil/compost/gravel mix to build up a level for the next layer of rocks. These should be stepped back from the lowest course. Fill the cavities between the rocks and in them with the topsoil mixture, but keep the rocks close together so that they don't appear lost in a sea of topsoil.

Continue in this way, building up the tiers of the rockery in gradually smaller V-sections until you reach the top which should be finished off with a single large rock or a group of smaller ones.

After planting the rockery, spread more gravel around and between the plants to disguise the soil and help retain moisture.

Dry stream beds

One effective way to use stone in a garden is to construct a dry stream bed which can make an ideal division between two elements of the garden. Ideally, it should run along the bottom of a slope or possibly at the foot of a retaining wall.

The dry stream bed is relatively easy to construct and can be as wide as you like, although it should not be too narrow as that would reduce its visual impact.

To construct the bed, mark out its course using pegs and cord, or thick rope or hose laid on the ground. Remember, you are trying to create the impression of a meandering stream, so keep the curves gentle and sweeping. Dig out the topsoil to a depth of about 100mm (4in) and compact the subsoil by treading it down, rolling it, or ramming it down with a heavy piece of wood. Treat the foundation liberally with weedkiller to prevent weeds growing up through the bed. Then spread a 75mm (3in) layer of sand over the bottom, raking it out level.

The stream bed should be formed from a layer of flat pebbles spread over the sand so that they are level with the sides. Then place a few larger rounded rocks in groups of two or three, and occasionally singly to break up the uniformity of the pebble surface.

The effect can be completed by setting larger irregularly shaped rocks along the "banks" of the stream and planting between them.

Where a path has to cross the dry stream bed, you could either set paving stones or flat-topped rocks into the surface to act as stepping stones, or build a small bridge from wood set on brick piers (see page 90). One effective way of doing this is to use old railway sleepers/railroad ties, staggering the bridge at mid stream by laying the ends of two sleepers/ties side by side on an extra-wide pier.

Rock beds

If you don't think you can cope with the problems of building a true rockery, you can use the dry-stream bed construction method to make an attractive rock bed for planting alpines. This should be laid out flat on the ground and covered with a layer of coarse stone chips. Arrange a few larger stones strategically and then add the plants.

(Above) The more common form of rockery with stones arranged haphazardly and no attempt made to create the appearance of a natural rocky outcrop. Even so, such rockeries can be attractive if the stones are arranged to make the most of their own individual decorative properties.

(Below) The latter is the case in this rock bed where the stones are gradually being submerged by the vigorously growing plants. Stones for this particular type of rockery need not be particularly large and should be set out in the most visually attractive pattern as a rugged contrast to the delicacy of the blooms and foliage.

Japanese style

For centuries the Japanese have made clever use of stone in all forms in their gardens, and they use it in a manner that makes the most of the stone's texture and shape and goes beyond seeing the material as something purely functional.

Japanese style gardens have a simplicity that produces an air of tranquility. They are ideal for relaxing in, providing a place for contemplation. Their style is also particularly suitable for small walled courtyards. Or you could build such a garden within a much larger one, perhaps instead of a patio adjacent to the house.

One feature found in many Japanese style gardens is the use of coarse gravel or stone chips to form a "sea" that spreads across most of the ground. Indeed, it effectively replaces the lawn that is so common in Western gardens and is a much better idea than the tiny lawns so often found in smaller gardens.

Such a gravel "sea" could be laid directly on to a compacted subsoil base, but would be better on a 50mm (2in) layer of sand. The gravel or stone chips should be spread out to a thickness of about 75mm (3in).

Large flat-topped rocks can be set in this "sea" as stepping stones, rather than having a solid path, or you could use paving slabs, preferably not a rectangular shape. Heavy wooden sections, suitably treated with preservative, such as old railway sleepers/railroad ties, can

The Japanese make very effective use of stone in all its forms in their gardens, seeing it as having decorative properties in its own right. Many lessons can be learned from them in this respect.
(Above) Individual rocks and plants are grouped together like small islands in a "sea" of stone chips in this garden. The hollowed stone acts as a tsukubai, *the traditional washing bowl that forms part of the Japanese tea ceremony. Normally, water flows continuously from the bowl and a ladle may be placed across it for drinking.*
(Right) Gravel and stone chips feature prominently in Japanese gardens and it is quite common for large areas to be spread out and raked into swirling patterns. Individual and small groups of rocks are arranged as islands in the "sea" of chips, while moss is often grown around them.
(Far right) Very large stones and rocks will be positioned to provide a focal point for the garden in much the same way as statues or sculptures.

also be used to form a pathway.

Additional rocks with interesting shapes should be set like small rocky islands in the stone "sea" with a planting of moss or some other ground cover plant around their bases.

To finish it off the gravel should be raked into swirling patterns around the rocks with straight lines in between them using a rake with very wide prongs. In fact, you might have to make a simple rake for this, cutting a series of zig-zag

"teeth" in the edge of a board fixed to the end of a broom handle.

The oriental "feel" to this sort of garden could be emphasized by the careful placing of Japanese style urns or lanterns and by restricting planting to a few, carefully selected plants and small shrubs.

A water feature could be added in the form of a *tsukubai*, which is a hollowed rock "bowl," into which a constant flow of water trickles from a bamboo spout. With a bit of ingenuity, it would not be too difficult to arrange this using a waterfall pump.

SPECIAL FEATURES

This section looks at some of the most popular and interesting garden features – arches, pergolas, trellises, screens, play areas, storage units – that can be simply and effectively constructed from brick, stone or wood. Some of them, such as pergolas and trellises, can combine well with walls and fencing, both of which are explored fully in earlier sections of the book.

Throughout your garden there will be a need for many special types of features and in building them you can give your imagination free rein, tailoring them exactly to meet the needs of your family and to fit in with the overall style of your garden.

In some cases a special feature may have a purely decorative aspect, such as an archway linking one part of the garden with another, or it might have a more practical purpose, such as a trellis to provide a support for climbing plants or a screen to provide a little shade on a patio.

Sometimes it is necessary to devise a means of disguising the more unsightly but necessary elements of the garden, such as a shed, rubbish containers or a heating-oil storage tank. Or you may simply want to make the garden a little more fun for your children by creating their own special play area.

Constructing an area of the garden especially for children should be embarked upon only after consideration of the overall design of the whole garden. Here, the "oriental style" simply but effectively extends into a practical, semi-enclosed section where children can play safely for hours.

Arches

Wooden arches can be given many forms to match the style of your garden.
*(**Below**) A simple framework with panels of trellis provides the ideal support for climbing plants which will soon cover the framework completely.*

A wooden archway is an appealing means of linking one part of the garden with another, particularly if the two areas are separated by a fence or hedge. It can be practical, too, providing support for climbing plants that, in time, will disguise the presence of the wooden framework completely.

You can build various styles of arch, depending on the style of your garden. In a country garden, you might choose to build the arch from rustic poles with the bark still in place; for a more formal garden, you could build a structure from square planed timbers or even erect "pillars" with square sections of wood at their corners and panels of trellis in between, the entire arch being painted white. For an arch leading from an oriental style part of the garden you could use large sections of wood with a single crosspiece at the top, its ends cut at an angle sloping upward. In fact, whatever the style of your garden, you should be able to devise a style of arch that will fit in with it.

Building an arch
Regardless of type, a wooden arch is relatively straightforward to build, and in most cases the various wooden sections are simply held together with galvanized nails.

It is a good idea to sketch out your ideas on paper first. Then take photographs of the archway's position from both sides and use tracing paper to produce overlays that will show what your ideas will look like when built. As a guide, an arch should give about 2.4m (8ft) of headroom and be at least 1.2m (4ft) wide. When you are happy with the design, you can order the materials.

As a rule wood with a diameter or width of 75–100mm (3–4in) will be needed for the main supporting framework of an arch. If possible, softwood should be purchased already pressure-treated with preservative, but if this is not available you can treat it yourself by brushing preservative on. Make sure you stand the feet of the uprights in buckets of preservative for several days so that it really soaks into the endgrain. Rustic

poles with the bark left in place should only be treated on their ends as the bark will prevent absorption of the preservative.

In many cases, no fabricated joints will be necessary to assemble the sections of the arch since there will be little loading on them. The pieces can simply be overlapped and nailed, or their ends formed into halving joints by removing half of the wood for a distance equal to the width of the piece being joined to it, using a small saw.

Depending on the style of arch, probably the best method of construction is to assemble end frames comprising a pair of uprights and the necessary crosspieces. Then dig holes for the uprights to a depth of about 450mm (1ft 6in). Place a layer of hardcore in the bottoms of the holes, stand the frames in place and support them temporarily with pairs of stakes driven into the ground at an angle, as you would a fence post (see page 28). Wedge the feet of the uprights with more hardcore and then set them with a collar of concrete, trowelling it off so that rainwater will run away from the feet of the posts.

Leave the concrete to set for about a week, then nail on the sections of wood joining the two end frames. These can be plain horizontal lengths of wood or diagonal crosspieces.

(Left) Rustic poles are a favourite for arches. The natural appearance of the poles blends well with any informal setting. Special joints are not needed; the poles are simply nailed together, using stout uprights and thinner braces.

Pergolas

Pergolas are ideal for shading a walkway and providing support for climbing plants. (*Right*) As with arches, rustic poles are ideal for constructing pergolas, and a simple framework such as this is all that is needed. The tops of the uprights are joined by poles running the length of the pergola, and crosspieces are added to provide a "roof." If necessary, wires can be stretched between the crosspieces for training plants, but don't overdo it, otherwise you will create a dark tunnel when the plants have grown fully. (*Below*) Here is a much sturdier looking pergola with piers of split stone and substantial wooden beams. The stone piers match the crazy paving of the path and the whole has a well established look. The important thing to remember when constructing a pergola is to keep it in scale with your garden.

Whether attached to the house wall, or a boundary wall or freestanding, pergolas are an attractive means of providing shade to a walkway or patio as well as support for climbing plants. They are invariably built from wood, although some may have brick or block columns supporting heavy section wooden crosspieces. Taut wires may be strung between the crosspieces to provide extra support for plants, or rails may be added to form a latticework "roof." The uprights, whether of wood or masonry, can have more wires strung between them, or trellis panels added, or even screen blocks if the supporting columns are of masonry.

As with arches, pergolas can be built in many styles to suit varying types of garden, so it should not be too difficult to come up with something that fits in exactly with your own plot. Once again,

it is a good idea to take photographs of the area where the pergola is to be built and use tracing paper overlays to try out various designs until you find the right one.

Similar sizes of wood should be used for a pergola as for an arch and the minimum width and headroom apply also.

Building a lean-to pergola

With a lean-to pergola attached to a house wall or boundary wall in the garden, the crosspieces at the top are supported at their inner ends by a length of wood screwed to the wall (known as a wall plate) and at their outer ends by upright poles or masonry piers. In addition, there will normally be a rail running the length of the pergola, tying the tops of the uprights together – if they are made from wood.

The wall plate will normally be installed first – you can attach it to the wall with long screws and plastic wall plugs or use expanding bolts/expansion shields if it is a heavy section. Next, dig holes for the posts and set in concrete in the same manner used to erect fence posts; allow the concrete to harden fully

(Above) The framework of a pergola not only provides a suitable support for climbing plants but can also be used for hanging baskets, which is a good idea while you are waiting for climbing plants to grow.
(Above left) This starkly simple pergola provides visual impact in what would otherwise be a very open garden.

Pergolas

This simple arch and framework constructed from rustic poles shows how effective this material can be. Its attraction lies in its natural appearance and the ease with which frameworks can be erected. The bark will provide protection against the weather, so only the ends of the poles need to be treated with preservative.

before building the rest of the structure.

The crosspieces can be notched at the inner ends so that they rest on top of the wall plate, then secured by galvanized nails or brass screws, while at the outer ends they can be nailed or screwed to the sides of the posts. The rails can be nailed or screwed to the outer faces of the posts.

Where masonry uprights are chosen, the crosspieces and wall plate should be of substantial section so as not to look out of scale. Crosspieces can be attached to the uprights by either screwing or bolting them to the sides of the uprights or by attaching them to the tops using simple L-shaped steel brackets.

Erecting a freestanding pergola

Erecting a freestanding pergola follows the procedure for a wooden archway. Individual arch frames are nailed together and set in holes in the ground with concrete collars. When the concrete has set additional crosspieces and rails can be added to tie the structure together.

Similar techniques can be used to erect a gazebo, although the "roof" timbers would meet in the middle (possibly being fixed to a central block) and pitched upward for improved appearance.

(**Above**) You will need surprisingly few tools and materials to construct an arch or pergola using rustic poles. Although the construction must be sound, accuracy is not quite as essential as it would be with wood of uniform section. Slight variations in the sizes and arrangement of the frame's pieces are all part of the attraction of the final appearance.

(**Above**) One way in which the uprights can be fixed firmly in the ground is to use land-drain pipes/drain tiles as sockets. These are set in concrete as you would a normal fence post, checking carefully that they are upright. Then, once you have treated the feet of the posts with preservative, they can be inserted in the pipes and secured with a mortar collar, trowelled off to a slope.

(**Above**) Although the poles can simply be overlapped and nailed together, you can make more secure joints by removing half of each adjoining pole so that they fit together snugly. Simply saw halfway through the pole at the end of each joint and remove the waste with a sharp chisel. These particular cutouts will fit over the tops of the uprights.

(**Above**) Once the mortar securing the uprights has set, you can add the crosspieces, fitting the cutouts over the ends of the poles and nailing down through them. Drill clearance holes for the nails through the crosspieces to prevent them from splitting when the nails are driven through.

(**Above**) Where you want to incorporate a continuous rail running the length of the pergola, you will have to join shorter lengths of pole. The joints should always be in an upright position to ensure adequate support for the joint, and the ends of the poles should be cut as shown. Drill clearance holes through each and drive a nail through both poles into the upright.

(**Above**) Diagonal braces should be added between the uprights and horizontal rails for added strength. Cut the ends of the braces at the appropriate angle and drill clearance holes for the nails. When driving a nail up into a horizontal rail, hold a heavy weight on top, such as the end of a sledgehammer, to prevent the rail from being lifted from the tops of the uprights.

Screens

Although sitting in the sun can be very pleasant, you can have too much of a good thing, and there are times when a shady spot is called for. Some plants do not appreciate being in the sun all day either – in fact, some plants don't like the sun at all. So if your garden does not have any naturally shady areas, it is a good idea to create some. One way is to erect some form of screen that will allow sunlight to filter through but create enough shade to provide comfortable conditions for both people and plants.

Normally screens are erected as part of a pergola or similar structure bordering a patio, being fixed between the supporting uprights. However, there is no reason why they should not be constructed as a form of fence between normal fence posts.

One very popular type of screen is the trellis, a latticework of narrow wooden or plastic slats – about 25 × 13mm /(1 × ½in) – forming open squares about 150mm (6in) in size. Trellis panels can be bought ready-made, but it is not difficult to make them. The slats are simply nailed together and can be attached to a supporting framework of larger-section battens at the edges. These can then be nailed between wooden uprights and plants encouraged to climb up the open framework. In fact, with a trellis screen, it is really the plants that provide the shade since the very open nature of the structure provides very little shade on its own.

The trellis has many uses around the garden as a plant support. It can be added to the tops of fences, fixed to walls, used to build pillars for ornamental arches, and even employed to clad the framework for an arbour containing a seat.

Trellises are a versatile form of screening.
(Above) Here, the weathered trellis merges into the background as the brightly coloured plants focus the eye.
(Below) In this instance, the trellis is a feature in its own right.

(Above) A trellis has been used to good effect here to provide screening to one side of a weathered brick and wood pergola. While allowing the rest of the garden to be viewed, it focuses the eye on the immediate foreground.

(Left) Climbing plants can be used to form an attractive natural screen and the simplest support for them is wire mesh attached to a sturdy wooden frame.

(Below, far left) Split cane is effective screening material, providing shade yet letting sunlight and light breezes filter through.

(Below left) Trellises can be used to extend the height of a fence without producing a solid barrier which would rob the garden of sunlight.

Another means of forming a screen is to use larger wooden slats, say $38 \times 18mm/1\frac{1}{2} \times \frac{3}{4}$in, and nail them to an outer framework fixed between posts so that the slats are either vertical or horizontal. They should be spaced at least 25mm (1in) apart, or nailed on alternate sides of the edge battens so that you can't see directly through them but light can filter in diagonally between the slats.

For more solid screens, panels of reeds or split bamboo secured by wire can be fixed between the uprights of a pergola or between fence posts, as can woven hurdles.

Play areas

Although it is extremely difficult to confine children to one particular area of the garden, you may want to make the garden more fun for them by providing an area with one or two items of play equipment where they can work off some of their energy. A sandbox and climbing frame are both relatively easy to construct yet will provide hours of fun and possibly save some of the rest of the garden from the ravages of bicycles and footballs – at least for part of the time.

Building a sandbox
Sandboxes can be built from masonry or wood, and in the former case, if you are careful with the design, you may be able to convert it to a pond at a later date when the children have grown up.

Although a sandbox is easier to build above ground level, if the edges are wide enough to sit on, consider sinking it into the ground, as this will prevent injuries should a child topple back off the edge. This is not so critical if the box is surrounded by grass, but is important if it is set in a paved surface.

For a wooden-framed sandbox, use something like $38 \times 225mm/1\frac{1}{2} \times 9in$ untreated boards, fixed in pairs one on top of the other to 100mm (4in) square uprights set in the ground at 900mm (3ft) intervals. Do *not* use pressure-treated wood because of the preservative's possible toxicity and its proximity to children. Line the floor of the sandbox with bricks, pavers or paving slabs laid on a foundation of hardcore and sand as you would when laying a path or patio (see page 36). Don't fill the joints in the paving as this ensures rapid drainage of the box during rainy weather. Fill the box with fine, washed sand.

By enlarging the perimeter framework of this type of box and adding a supporting framework of $100 \times 50mm/4 \times 2in$ sections you can deck one end with $150 \times 25mm/6 \times 1in$ boards and use it as a seating area or a play table.

One important point to keep in mind when constructing wooden play equipment is to make sure the wood is sanded thoroughly to prevent any likelihood of the children picking up splinters.

For a masonry sandbox, build it as you would a raised pond with dwarf walls around the edges and overlapping concrete slab coping/cap stones. The floor can be slabs or pavers laid on a hardcore and sand foundation to aid drainage. When the children grow up, this structure can be converted to a pond by emptying out the sand, removing the paving and its foundation, and installing a flexible pond liner. The coping/cap stones will need to be removed and rebedded to secure the edges of the liner, but if only a little mortar was used for this job in the first place, this should not be too difficult to do.

A simple climbing frame
Any climbing frame must be very sturdy to stand up to the bashing it will receive from children intent on having a good time. Although you can build quite complex structures, it is probably just as well to keep it simple. Its size will depend on the age of the children who are to use it, which is probably another good reason for keeping it simple, as they will soon outgrow it.

One method of construction is to build a small bridge with ladder-like end frames and a connecting walkway complete with handrails. For the main frame use $100 \times 50mm/4 \times 2in$ wood and $100 \times 25mm/4 \times 1in$ wood for the slats and ladder rungs. The width of such a frame should be about 500mm (1ft 8in) and its span about 1.2m (4ft).

The walkway can be built by cutting two lengths of main frame material and nailing or screwing slats across it with 13mm ($\frac{1}{2}$in) gaps in between. The rails should project beyond the end slats by about 150mm (6in).

The ladder sections should have side pieces made from the main frame material with the treads fixed between them on triangular blocks of wood 50mm (2in) wide by 50mm (2in) deep screwed to the side pieces. The treads are then screwed to the triangular blocks. The width of the ladder sections is such that they fit inside the rails of the walkway and continue upward to provide a fixing for a $100 \times 50mm/4 \times 2in$ handrail on each side. Each ladder section is attached to the walkway at an angle of about 60 degrees, using two carriage bolts per side to prevent them splaying out.

(Above) A simple climbing frame can be made from wood in the form of a bridge. The slatted bridge piece is fixed with carriage bolts to angled ladder sections (the lengths of which can be designed to suit yourself) and the sides of the ladders are extended upward to provide fixings for handrails.

(Far left) Children enjoy playing with sand, and a simple sandbox can be made from wood as shown here. The overlapping edge boards can be used for sitting on. Being set low in the gravel surround removes any possibility of injury should a child trip and fall.

(Left) This sandbox has been neatly incorporated into the corner of a wooden decked patio. The wide sections of wood provide both seating and a means of containing the sand.

Storage units and camouflage

No matter how neat the garden, there will always be some features that you would rather not see – rubbish containers, a compost heap, an old potting shed. You can't do without these items, but you can improve their appearance by either building a storage unit around them or by disguising them with some form of screening.

For items such as garbage containers some form of simple U-shaped screen can be built from pierced screen concrete walling blocks or some other type of masonry, such as brick or reconstituted stone block. Alternatively, a low fence could be built around them, and if this were panelled with trellis, plants could be allowed to climb up it to make the disguise a natural one.

If a masonry wall was chosen, it could also be roofed in with a simple wooden framework clad with exterior-grade plywood panels and covered with roofing felt. The roof structure could be attached to the walls with screws or with metal brackets.

Many other unsightly features of your garden can be treated in the same way, trellis being particularly suitable for disguising larger items such as heating-oil

(Above) Wood stacks can be untidy, but this storage unit solves the problem neatly and doubles as seating. Furthermore, being under the porch, the wood can be reached in all weather.

(Right) There are many items kept outdoors that are unattractive, among them garbage cans and fuel. A brick-built store such as this provides concealment and keeps fuel dry. The doors are made simply of wood, while the roof is panelled in wood with a covering of roofing felt.

tanks and garden sheds. You may only need a single flat screen, or perhaps an L-shaped one built around two sides of the offending item.

A compost heap is essential for any keen gardener, allowing plant debris to be disposed of and recycled by returning it to the soil after it has broken down into a good growing medium. However, an untidy heap in a corner of the garden may not fit into the overall scheme of things. Again, a screen could be built to conceal it, but a better idea is to build a proper compost bin.

A simple compost bin can be constructed from four 100mm (4in) square posts set in the ground to a depth of about 450mm (1ft 6in) with concrete collars and standing about 900mm (3ft) high. They should be spaced about 900mm (3ft) apart. Wooden slats, measuring 75 × 25mm/1 × 3in should be nailed at 50mm (2in) intervals across the back and sides. The gaps between the slats allow the necessary circulation of air through the heap to speed up decomposition.

You need to make the slats removable at the front so that you can dig out the compost when it is ready. The easiest

way is to nail 75 × 13mm/3 × ½in wood pieces to the sides of the posts, leaving 25mm (1in) horizontal slots in between and allowing the front slats to be pushed in on edge.

Although you could manage with one compost bin, for series use you will need three – one that you are filling, one that you are taking compost from, and the third that is full of decomposing plant waste. By building them in a block you will only need eight posts. You may also be able to manage with only two sets of removal slats since you are unlikely to need all three bins closed off at once.

(Right) In a small garden such as this, a solid fence erected across one section will provide a screen behind which garbage cans can be hidden. If you grow plants along the fence and in front of it, it too will eventually "disappear."
(Below) Although not hiding these bins completely, this storage unit does a good job of making them less obtrusive, yet at the same time keeping them readily accessible. The cast concrete "roof" has been used as the base for a simple planter with a surround of bricks.

Concrete and Mortar

Construction work in your garden invariably requires the use of concrete or mortar. Concrete particularly has many applications, especially as a foundation for garden walls and other structures, as a reinforcement for fence posts, and even as a paving material in its own right. Mortar is essential for building masonry walls and can also be used for bedding various types of paving.

Both materials are based on a mixture of cement and sand, with the former also including a mixture of gravel or crushed stone. When mixed with water, the cement in both concrete and mortar reacts to bind the ingredients into a dense, hard mass that is immensely strong.

Concrete and mortar take some time to harden, full strength not being achieved for about a month; but, usually after about a week, it will have achieved half strength, which is sufficient to begin to build on.

You can buy the ingredients of concrete and mortar separately and mix them yourself, or you can buy them premixed in convenient bags which are ideal for small jobs. For a really big concreting job, you can either rent a powered mixer or have the concrete delivered ready-mixed, ready for laying.

Concrete

Concrete is a mixture of cement, sharp or concreting sand, and coarse and fine aggregate (crushed stone or gravel). Depending on the strength required, these are mixed in different proportions (see table on page 117) with water.

Mixing concrete

Mixing concrete can be heavy work, especially if you have a lot of concreting to do, so it is worth renting a mixer if possible. For hand mixing you will need two buckets and two shovels, keeping one of each purely for the cement – don't allow these to come into contact with any water as the cement on them will harden and you will begin to set off a reaction with your supply of cement which will soon make it useless.

First, measure out the required amount of sand and aggregate using the buckets and arrange it in a heap on your mixing surface (which must be clean and dry) with a crater in the middle. Add the required amount of cement to the crater and then begin to turn the heap with a shovel until it has a uniform gray colour.

Make another crater in the middle of the heap and add some water. Mix it in by adding dry material from the edge to the pool until it is absorbed. Turn the mix and repeat the process, carrying on until the concrete is well mixed. It should not be dry and crumbly, nor wet and sloppy, and it should hold the impression of your shovel if you use it to trowel off the top of the heap.

After mixing, concrete will remain workable for about two hours (less in hot weather), so have your site prepared and ready to receive the concrete as soon as you have finished mixing it. You can transport it to the site in a wheelbarrow.

Immediately after any concreting work, wash all your tools thoroughly to prevent the concrete from hardening on them.

Casting concrete slabs and strips

Although you can often lay concrete at the bottom of a trench, using the sides of the trench to contain it, in light crumbly soils or where a shallow slab of concrete

For small quantities of concrete or mortar it is worth buying ready-bagged ingredients, as these are easier to handle. Here, all-in aggregate (a mixture of sand and aggregate in the correct proportions for concreting) is being turned over to ensure that the ingredients are evenly mixed. Using a board for mixing will prevent damage to the surface of a patio, path, etc. Hand mixing is fine for small quantities, but for a large job consider renting a mixer or buying concrete ready-mixed.

Once the aggregate and sand are mixed thoroughly, the cement can be added in the required proportion. Use buckets of the same size to measure out the quantities, keeping one specifically for the cement. This must not become wet at all, otherwise it will trigger the chemical reaction that makes the cement harden. Turn the pile of cement, sand and aggregate over to mix it thoroughly.

is required at ground level, you will need to construct wooden formwork to contain the concrete while it sets.

Formwork for concreting is easy to set up. You need wooden boards that are as wide as the slab is thick (including any layer of hardcore) and some 50mm (2in) square wooden stakes.

After digging out the topsoil, drive the stakes in around the perimeter of the proposed slab and nail the boards to their inner faces, making sure the tops of the boards are perfectly level. The stakes should not protrude above the level of the boards.

If laying concrete over a layer of hardcore, spread this over the site and ram it down well, but take care not to disturb the formwork. Then add the concrete, spread it out with a rake until it is just above the level of the formwork, and work it into the corners.

Next tamp the concrete, using a 50mm (2in) thick wooden beam. Work it up and down with a chopping motion at first to spread the concrete out and then go back over the slab with a sawing motion, striking the concrete off level with the top of the formwork.

If the concrete is to be exposed as some form of paving, you can give it various textured finishes by dragging a stiff-bristled broom across it, by smooth-

Keep turning the materials over until the pile has a uniform gray colour and there are no pockets of unmixed cement left anywhere. Then form a crater in the centre of the pile with your shovel. Build up the sides so that when you add the water it cannot escape.

(Top) Add some water to the crater – you will find using a watering can for this makes the job easier – and gradually feed the dry concrete mix into it, working your way around the pile. When the water has been absorbed, turn the mix over and form another crater. Add more water and continue in this way until the concrete is mixed thoroughly.
(Above) Work your shovel across the mixed concrete with an angled chopping motion – the mix should retain the shovel marks.

Concrete and Mortar

A concrete base makes a good foundation for almost all outside building work.

The first step is to work out the area, and it is better to err on the generous side. After digging out the surface soil, fix the formwork (**see left**) to pegs driven into the ground. Make sure the tops of the boards are level. A foundation of hardcore is then firmed in before barrowing in the concrete and compacting and levelling it with a tamping beam (**left**). The forms should be left in position for about a week.

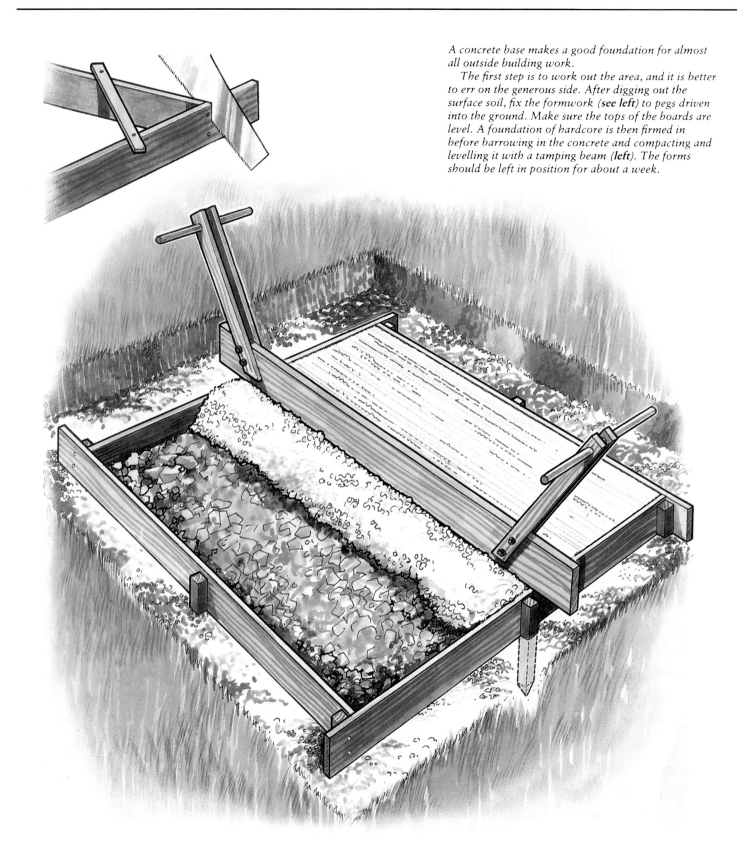

Concrete mixing ratios

Mix		Sand	Aggregate	Cement	UK only All-in aggregate
General purpose	UK	2	$2\frac{1}{2}$–3	1	4
	US	2	4	1	–
Foundation	UK	2–$2\frac{1}{2}$	3–$3\frac{1}{2}$	1	5
	US	2–$2\frac{1}{2}$	5	1	–
Paving	UK	$1\frac{1}{2}$	$2\frac{1}{2}$	1	$3\frac{1}{2}$
	US	2	3	1	–

ing it in a circular motion with the back of your shovel, or by polishing it with a trowel. If you allow the concrete to stiffen for a while and then go over it with a broom and watering can you can expose the aggregate in it for an attractive finish.

After about a week the formwork can be removed.

Mortar

Although outwardly similar to concrete, mortar needs different types of the same basic ingredients. The cement should be proper masonry cement and the sand mixed with it soft or builder's sand. The latter makes the mortar more workable and "buttery." The cement and sand should be mixed in the proportion of 1 part cement (Type N in US) to $4\frac{1}{2}$/3 parts sand. Prepacked dry mortar mix is often a good way of buying the materials, rather than in bulk, since you are only likely to use relatively small amounts at a time, and if the mix is already bagged up it will make storage a lot easier.

Special white cement and coloured pigments are also available to make the mortar's appearance match that of the masonry being used.

Mortar is mixed in much the same way as concrete, the dry materials being thoroughly combined first, and then water added to a crater until it is completely mixed in. It is best to mix up small amounts at a time – no more than you can use in an hour. It should have the consistency of butter that is soft enough to spread with a knife.

Using mortar

Carry the mortar to your job in a bucket and tip it out on to a clean board. Work it into shape with a bricklayer's trowel so that you can scoop up a trowel load easily. This is done by separating some from the rest using a sawing motion with the trowel blade, at the same time moving the blade in an arc to round off the back edge of the mortar slice. Then slide the blade under the mortar from the front and lift it from the board.

To lay a bed of mortar, hold the trowel directly over the spot where it is to be laid, tilting it downward and sliding it back at the same time so that the mortar slips off the blade into place. Furrow the mortar with the tip of the trowel to spread it out into an even layer for bedding a brick or block.

INDEX

ACKNOWLEDGMENTS

The majority of the photographs reproduced in this book were supplied by
Elizabeth Whiting & Associates.

Front cover, Linda Burgess/Insight; p.6–7, Matthew Stevens; 9, 10R, Debra Wetherley/EWA; 11T, Jerry Tubby/EWA; 12B, 14TL, EWA; 14TR, David Secombe; 15R, EWA; 17T, Ann Kelley/EWA; 17B, Hans Verkroost; 19T, 19B, Hans Verkroost; 20, David Ward; 21T, EWA; 21BL, David Secombe; 21BR, David Ward; 22TR, Hans Verkroost; 23, EWA; 25, EWA; 26L/C/R, 27BL, Hans Verkroost; 27BR, 28, EWA; 29T, Karl Dietrich Buhler/EWA; 29B, Michael Dunne/EWA; 30, David Secombe; 31TL, EWA; 31BL, Jerry Tubby/EWA; 31TR/BR, Ann Kelley/EWA; 32, EWA; 33T/BL/BR, Ann Kelley/EWA; 35, Jerry Harpur; 36L/C/R, 37, EWA; 38T Hans Verkroost; 38B, Gary Chowanetz/EWA; 39T, Matthew Stevens; 39BL, Hans Verkroost; 39BR, David Secombe; 40L, Hans Verkroost; 40C, Spike Powell/EWA; 40R, EWA; 41, Peter Woloszynski/EWA; 42L, Matthew Stevens; 42R, 43L, David Secombe; 43R, Friedhelm Thomas/EWA; 44L/R, 45T, EWA; 45B, Neil Lorimer/EWA; 46TL/TC/TR, EWA; 46B, David Secombe; 47L/R, EWA; 48T, Friedhelm Thomas/EWA; 48B, Hans Verkroost; 49, David Secombe; 51, Di Lewis/EWA; 52TL/TC/TR/B, 53T/B, 54TR, Hans Verkroost; 54B 55, 56, EWA; 57T, Karl Dietrich Buhler/EWA; 57B, Matthew Stevens; 59, EWA; 60T, Hans Verkroost; 60B, David Secombe; 61, 62L/R, 63TL/TC/TR, EWA; 63B David Secombe; 64T/B, 65T/BL/BR, EWA; 65T, Jerry Tubby/EWA; 67, David Secombe; 68T/C, Matthew Stevens; 68B, 69L, 70T/B, David Secombe; 71T, John Miller; 71B, 72T/B, 73T/B, 74, 74–5, David Secombe; 75L, Karl Dietrich Buhler/EWA; 75R, David Secombe; 76B, Spike Powell/EWA; 77T/B, EWA; 79, Michael Dunne/EWA; 80, 81T, EWA; 81B, David Secombe; 82T, Matthew Stevens; 82C, EWA; 82B, Rodney Hyett/EWA; 84TL/TC/TR/BL/BCL/BCR/BR, 85T/BL/BR, EWA; 86, David Secombe; 87T/B, John Miller; 88L, David Secombe; 88R, Julian Nieman/EWA; 89, EWA; 90, Karl Dietrich Buhler/EWA; 91TL, EWA; 91TR/B, David Secombe; 93, 94, 95, EWA; 96T, Hans Verkroost; 96B, EWA; 97T, Hans Verkroost; 97B, EWA; 98, 98–9, 99, Japan National Tourist Organization; 101, Karl Dietrich Buhler/EWA; 102, 103, EWA; 104T/B, 105B, David Secombe; 105T, 106, 107TL/TC/TR/BL/BC/BR, 108T, EWA; 108B, Michael Dunne/EWA; 109TL, Karl Dietrich Buhler/EWA; 109TR, Matthew Stevens; 109BL, Hans Verkroost; 109BR, Ceri Norman; 110, Friedhelm Thomas/EWA; 111B Frank Herholdt/EWA; 112T, Spike Powell/EWA; 112B, Jerry Tubby/EWA; 113T, EWA; 113BL, Spike Powell/EWA; 113BR, Jerry Tubby/EWA; 114L/R, 115TL/TR/B, EWA.

Illustrations 10L, 11B, 12–13T, 13B, © Uitgeverij het Spectrum B.V. 1974; 8, 18, 22, 24, 34, 50, 58, 66, 76T, 78, 92, 100, Nigel Jones; 54TL, 111T, 116, John Hutchinson.